BIRDS OF THE
PUGET SOUND REGION
COAST TO CASCADES

By

Dennis Paulson
Bob Morse
Tom Aversa
Hal Opperman

R.W. Morse Company
Olympia, Washington

For Netta (D.P.)
For Christina (B.M.)
For Cheryl (T.A.)
For JoLynn (H.O.)

Published by R.W. Morse Company, Olympia, Washington

Library of Congress Control Number: 2016902337
EAN 9780964081017 $24.95 Softcover
First Edition 2016   © 2016 R.W. Morse Company
Third Printing 2019

Revised and expanded from *Birds of the Puget Sound Region* (R.W. Morse Company, 2003)

Printed: China, Imago USA

Authors: Dennis Paulson, Bob Morse, Tom Aversa, and Hal Opperman

Executive Editor: Christina Duchesne Morse

Editor: Dennis Paulson

Photo Editor: Brian E. Small

Covers and Interior Design: Christina Merwin

Map: Darla Ashford

Cover Photographs: Brian E. Small
Front: Rufous Hummingbird
Back: Black Oystercatcher

Quick Guide to Local Birds

This guide is organized by families so related species are shown together. The Species Account pages are color-coded and thumb-indexed by bending the book edge to take you to a section.

Contents

Common Local Birds

Here are some of the most common birds in western Washington. For more information about each bird, go to its Species Account.

Surf Scoter
p. 63

Bufflehead
p. 69

Horned Grebe
p. 99

Canada Goose
p. 31

Mew Gull
p. 215

American Wigeon
p. 39

Glaucous-winged Gull
p. 225

Mallard
p. 41

Double-crested Cormorant p. 113

Red-tailed Hawk p. 141

Steller's Jay p. 303

Rock Pigeon p. 231

Anna's Hummingbird p. 257

Great Blue Heron p. 121

Downy Woodpecker p. 267

Northern Flicker p. 271

American Coot p. 149

American
Crow
p. 307

Black-capped
Chickadee
p. 323

Chestnut-backed
Chickadee
p. 327

Violet-green
Swallow
p. 315

Barn Swallow
p. 321

Bushtit
p. 329

Bewick's
Wren
p. 341

European Starling
p. 359

Red-breasted
Nuthatch
p. 331

Spotted Towhee
p. 385

Dark-eyed Junco
p. 403

American Robin
p. 355

House Finch
p. 429

American
Goldfinch
p. 435

Red-winged
Blackbird
p. 411

House Sparrow
p. 439

Song
Sparrow
p. 393

Introduction

Birding has become one of America's most popular outdoor activities. It is estimated that millions of people either watch or feed birds. Birding can be great family entertainment. It is easy to get started, inexpensive, healthy, and allows us to understand and appreciate the natural world.

Given the popularity of bird watching and the beauty of the Pacific Northwest, it is little wonder that the people of the Puget Sound Region enjoy seeing and studying our local birds. The region has a rich variety of bird life, with over 250 species of birds that are permanent residents or regular annual visitors to the 19 counties between the coast and mountains. These are the birds featured in this guide.

Birds of the Puget Sound Region: Coast to Cascades is for beginning birders who wish to know the birds of the greater Puget Sound area. This guide will also appeal to experienced birders who wish to learn more about the behavior, habitats, and seasonal occurrence of our local birds.

This fully revised and updated book covers the entire western half of Washington west of the Cascades Crest, from the Canadian border to the Columbia River. The term "region," as used in the guide, refers to this entire geographical area, as depicted on the map inside the front cover. The land portions of the region are those that drain toward both the Sound and the coast, from the crests of the Olympic Mountains and the Cascade Range to sea level. This book is for anyone interested in bird life in or near Seattle, Tacoma, Everett, Bellingham, Olympia, Chehalis, Aberdeen, Ocean Shores, Long Beach, Longview, Kelso, Vancouver, Bremerton, Mount Vernon, Port Angeles, and Port Townsend.

Identifying Birds

It can be confusing when you first start trying to identify birds. First, look at the general shape, size, and color of the bird. Check the Common Local Birds (pages vii–x) to see if it is there. If not, scan through the Species Account pages for your bird. Read the description—especially the **boldfaced** text—to see how it matches your bird. Compare range, similar species, and habitat. Keep comparing the bird to the book until you have a match.

The different colors of a bird's feathering ("plumage") and bare parts (bill, legs, feet) often provide the best ways to identify a bird. Most of the plumages and color patterns of each bird species are unique. However, plumages may vary within the same species between the sexes, between adults and younger birds, and by season.

In some species the male and the female have distinctly different plumages. Good examples are Mallard, House Finch, Red-winged Blackbird, and Rufous Hummingbird. Usually the males have the most brilliant colors, as in these examples, while the females have muted colors so they are not easily detected as they incubate eggs and raise young. Other species such as Rock Pigeon, Steller's Jay, American Crow, and Song Sparrow show no plumage differences between the sexes.

Most birds seen in the Puget Sound Region in spring and summer display what is known as their summer or "breeding" plumage. Birds seen here in winter are usually in their "nonbreeding" or winter plumage. Typically, but not always, the breeding plumage is more colorful or highly patterned and the nonbreeding plumage is more muted.

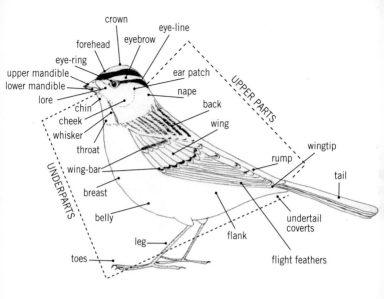

crown
eye-line
forehead
eyebrow
eye-ring
upper mandible
lower mandible
lore
ear patch
nape
chin
cheek
whisker
throat
back
wing
UPPER PARTS
wingtip
rump
tail
wing-bar
breast
belly
leg
toes
UNDERPARTS
flank
undertail coverts
flight feathers

Bird Drawing by Eric Kraig

Bird Anatomy. It is helpful to know the names of the different parts of a bird. This sketch of a White-crowned Sparrow shows the terms used to describe bird anatomy in this guide.

Molting is the process of replacing worn feathers with new, fresh feathers. Most local birds replace some or all of their feathers in a molt in fall when they change into their nonbreeding plumage. Most birds molt again in late winter or spring as they change into their breeding plumage. These molts occur over a period of several weeks or more.

Some birds have different plumages as they mature. This is particularly true for gulls, which take up to four years and several plumage stages to attain their adult plumage. The

3

term "juvenile plumage" refers to the plumage of a young bird after it loses its initial downy feathers. Some species hold this plumage for only a few weeks after fledging, while others may hold it into winter. "First-year plumage" is used for the plumage during the first 12 months of a bird's life. "Immature" refers to all plumages before the bird gains its adult plumage.

Color pattern may vary considerably among birds of the same species and plumage stage, especially when they belong to different geographic populations. For instance, Fox Sparrows that nest in the Cascades differ markedly in appearance from the ones that arrive to spend the winter in the lowlands of the Puget Sound Region. Differences can be great even within the same local population. In our region the majority of Red-tailed Hawks have light breasts and underwings, yet a certain percentage of birds have dark brown underparts and dark underwings with lighter-colored flight feathers. Such consistently different types are called "morphs."

In this book the birds are presented in family groupings, as shown in the Quick Guide to Local Birds on the first page inside the front cover. Beginning birders will find that learning the characteristics of the different bird families will make bird identification both easier and quicker. Birds in the same family look similar and often behave in a similar manner. Hummingbirds, for example, are all small, with long, thin bills, have fast wingbeats, and often hover. Once you see a bird with these characteristics, you are well on your way to identifying it as a hummingbird.

Don't expect every bird you see to look exactly like the photographs in this guide. Birds, like people, are individuals. To appreciate how variable birds of the same species can be, study the ones that come regularly to your backyard feeder.

Male House Finches, for example, can show a wide range of coloration from rich, deep red to golden yellow. You may find that with practice you can learn to recognize individual birds by the subtle differences in their markings.

Attracting Birds to Your Yard

Most people get involved in bird watching by observing the birds that appear in their yards. Perhaps the easiest way to see birds is to put up feeders and watch for birds to appear. When they are perched and eating, birds tend to stay long enough for you to study field marks at close range and identify them.

Although just hanging out a birdseed feeder will attract some birds, a complete backyard bird program has three important requirements: **food, water,** and **shelter**. By careful attention to all three of these elements you will not only increase the number and variety of birds that visit your yard, but you will also be contributing to their well-being. Many helpful books and brochures on bird feeding, nest boxes, and gardening for wildlife are available at nature stores and nurseries.

FOOD

The food that birds eat comes mainly from natural sources. Native and ornamental shrubs, trees, and other plants provide fruits, seeds, flowers, and insects. You will attract more birds to your yard by selecting plants favorable to birds.

You may also provide seed, suet, and other products to entice birds to your yard. Many seeds are suitable for feeding birds, although the best product in the Puget Sound Region is black-oil sunflower seed, which has high fat content. Many grocery and hardware stores sell a birdseed mix that contains some black-oil sunflower seed but often has a lot of millet (the small, round, tan-colored seed) and filler grains. When you place this seed in a hanging feeder five to six feet off the ground, some of the birds will eat only the sunflower seed and drop the filler and millet to the ground. In elevated feeders, it is much better to use only black-oil sunflower seed or a specialized mix that is high in nutritional value.

Different birds have different feeding preferences. You may wish to try more than one of the following common feeder types, depending on the species of birds you wish to attract.

- **Fly-through and hopper feeders** are hung or mounted on a pole or deck normally five to six feet above the ground. Stocked with black-oil sunflower seed, they attract Steller's Jays, finches, Red-breasted Nuthatches, chickadees, and grosbeaks.
- A **ground feeder or platform feeder** is placed near the ground or up to table height and filled with millet, corn, or a birdseed mix that has some black-oil sunflower seeds but is mostly millet. This feeder will attract doves, pigeons, ducks, sparrows, Dark-eyed Juncos, Spotted Towhees, and Red-winged Blackbirds. Buy a ground feeder with a bottom screen that allows the rain to drain through.
- Cylindrical **tube feeders** are either hung or mounted and can be filled with a nutritional mix of birdseed or just black-oil sunflower seed. They attract the smaller birds such as nuthatches, siskins, chickadees, and finches.
- A specialized tube feeder to hold Niger thistle seed is called a **thistle** or **finch feeder** and can attract numbers of finches such as House Finches, Pine Siskins, and American

Goldfinches.

- **Suet**, either acquired at a local meat market or purchased at the nature store in suet cakes, attracts woodpeckers, Red-breasted Nuthatches, chickadees, Bushtits, and a host of other birds seeking its high-energy fat.
- **Hummingbird feeders** attract Rufous and Anna's Hummingbirds that breed in the Puget Sound Region. It is easy to make hummingbird nectar: mix one part sugar to four parts water, boil, let cool, and then fill your feeders. Do not add any artificial food coloring; the red of the feeder is sufficient to attract hummingbirds.

Experiment with your feeder locations and different birdseed to learn what works best in your yard. Feeders should be placed close to natural shelters such as bushes and trees so the birds can escape from predators. You can feed the birds all year long without worrying that your bird feeding will delay the birds' fall migration. They will leave when the time is right.

Feeders, the ground below the feeders, and birdbaths need to be cleaned on a regular basis to eliminate the possibility of the spread of avian diseases. Scrub the feeders and birdbaths with soap and water. Mix one part bleach to ten parts hot water to sanitize them. Rinse them well then let them dry completely before refilling.

WATER

Birds need water for bathing and drinking. You will find that you attract more birds if you offer a reliable source of clean water in your yard. Consider placing a concrete birdbath filled with one inch of water to meet their needs. Clean and refill it regularly. Be sure the bottom surface is rough so the birds can get a good footing. Place the birdbath near shrubs or trees where they can preen after bathing and escape from predators. Try adding a dripper to the birdbath or getting a recirculating fountain. The sound of dripping water attracts birds.

SHELTER AND NEST BOXES

Birds need cover so they can seek protection from bad weather and predators. Nearby bushes, shrubs, and trees will help meet their needs as will a loosely stacked brush pile. Neighborhood cats can be a real problem, especially when they lurk beneath feeders and birdbaths. Careful placement or screening off of feeders and birdbaths, or placing chicken wire strategically in front of favorite cat stalking areas, will help protect the birds.

Some of the birds featured in this guide are cavity nesters and may be enticed to use a bird house which you can either build yourself or purchase at a nature store. It is important to realize that there is no such thing as a generic nest box. Different birds have different needs, and each nest box has to meet the demands of its occupant or it will not be used. The size of the opening and its height above the floor are critical, as is the height of the nest box above the ground. Some nest boxes also serve as wintering roosts for the smaller birds. It may take a season or two to attract chickadees, nuthatches, or swallows to your nest boxes.

Be sure to inspect nest boxes each fall and give them a good cleaning, but use no insecticides. Discard used nesting materials. Repair any damage so the boxes are ready and waiting for their new occupants to arrive in spring.

Observing Birds

Many bird watchers are content just to watch the birds in their yards casually. Some, however, get more involved and begin to look for birds beyond their immediate neighborhood. To get the most out of birding in the field, look and listen carefully and move slowly. Try to keep conversations to a minimum.

To help locate birds, watch for their movement and listen for their calls. Most often we see birds fly to a nearby branch or flit around in a tree. Their movement catches our attention. But an important part of bird watching is listening, and often it is its song or call that draws us to the bird.

Bird songs are a good way to identify birds. Each bird species has a unique song, and with practice you can learn to differentiate the songs. You can purchase CDs that allow you to study bird vocalizations at your leisure. With experience, you will be able to identify birds simply by their songs and calls.

WHEN TO GO BIRDING

Small birds tend to be most active when they are feeding early in the morning (as early as daybreak). Shorebirds tend to be most active while they are feeding on incoming and outgoing tides; they often roost away from feeding grounds at high tides. Hawks become active in the morning after the rising temperature creates thermals that lift them into the air. Most owls are nocturnal and are most active in the evening or just before dawn.

Puget Sound birds vary with the season. If you go out in different seasons, you will see different birds. Some species stay in the region throughout the year, while others arrive in the spring and leave in the fall. Other species migrate into the lowlands of our area from the north, the mountains, or the interior of the continent and spend the winter.

Spring is a great time of year. Flowers are blossoming, trees are getting their buds, and birds, in their bright breeding plumages, return from their wintering grounds. The males start singing and the local nesting birds seek mates, breed, and start to raise their families. Hummingbirds feed on flower nectar or at feeders. Wintering birds head north to their breeding grounds.

In summer the young birds hatch, and their parents are busy feeding them. As summer progresses, the young learn to fly and fend for themselves. By August, summer visitors are beginning to head south for their wintering grounds.

By late fall, the last Arctic-breeding shorebirds have passed through on their way south. As fall changes to winter, flocks of waterfowl appear on our lakes and ponds. Dunlins arrive to winter on local mudflats. Our resident birds continue to use neighborhood bird feeders, joined by winter visitors driven down to the lowlands by snowfall in the mountains.

WHERE TO GO BIRDING

As your birding interest and knowledge deepens, you will surely follow the path of most birders in wanting to see species beyond those that are in your yard. The Puget Sound Region is rich in bird habitats and bird species, and it is easy to see more and more of them just by increasing your range.

If you live in the suburbs or in the country, you probably already are surrounded by a great variety of bird species. If a city dweller, head for the larger parks. The larger the area of habitat, the more individual birds and the more species are likely to be present, so the parks are always richer than the more developed neighborhoods. All cities have such parks, for example Discovery Park and Magnuson Park in Seattle and Point Defiance Park in

Tacoma.

Water attracts birds, and the larger the water body, the more species are likely to be there. Suburban ponds may have only Mallards and Canada Geese, but a surprising number of ducks stop in such places if only briefly in migration. A Great Blue Heron or a kingfisher may take up residence if there is a good supply of fish. Larger ponds and lakes may feature the entire spectrum of freshwater birds, especially if there are beds of aquatic vegetation that shelter the birds' prey. Green Lake in Seattle and Capitol Lake in Olympia are wonderful places for birding in our big cities, and every county has lakes with public access that attract water birds.

Salt water has another set of species that rarely visit ponds and lakes in our region, so spend a lot of time at the ocean. The protected "inland" waters of the Strait of Juan de Fuca, the San Juan Islands, and Puget Sound harbor thousands of diving birds of many species, especially diving ducks, loons, grebes, cormorants, and alcids throughout the winter.

During that season, our diversity and abundance of seabirds is unequalled anywhere in the Lower 48. They can be seen from almost anywhere along the marine shoreline, and points that project from land allow especially good looks at these birds, some of them flying past at close range. A spotting scope is a valuable resource in these situations.

Deception Pass State Park and Libbey Beach Park offer good views of seabirds from Whidbey Island, as do Point No Point, Point Hudson and Point Wilson on the west side of Admiralty Inlet. Check out the protected bays at Ediz Hook off Port Angeles and road ends on Dungeness Bay. Walk out Dungeness Spit for a good combination of birding and exercise or take one of our numerous ferries to get a look at the seabirds that stay out in deep water.

The outer coast is especially productive during spring and fall migration, when tens of thousands of shorebirds, waterfowl, and shearwaters move through, some of them migrating from the Arctic to the tropics or farther. Ocean Shores and Westport, on either side of Grays Harbor, have jetties, beaches, and estuaries full of birds in season. For a real adventure, visit Cape Flattery and look out over Tatoosh Island; albatrosses have been seen from there.

KEEPING RECORDS

Some people keep a checklist of all the birds that appear in their yard ("yard list") or of all the birds seen in their lifetime ("life list"). As lists grow, so does a sense of personal accomplishment. Along with the pleasure of finding new and different birds comes an incentive to learn more about them. Many dedicated bird watchers keep a detailed journal of what they see, when and where, and the bird's behavior. Careful record keeping by knowledgeable observers can contribute greatly to scientific understanding of bird life. A checklist of the local birds is provided on pages 441-445.

Bird Habitats of Western Washington

The place where a bird or other living creature is normally found is termed its "habitat." Birds are quite diverse in their habitat requirements. Brown Creepers are seldom seen over open salt water or loons in trees. To a large extent, the secret to finding and identifying birds is knowing the habitats and developing an understanding of which birds are likely to be seen where. The more types of habitat you explore, the greater the variety of birds you will see.

The Puget Sound Region: Coast to Cascades features eleven major habitat categories:

1) OPEN SALT WATER

This habitat includes all marine waters of Washington: Puget Sound and adjoining inlets, bays, and straits, including the Strait of Juan de Fuca and the Strait of Georgia, as well as the outer coast. Our marine ecosystems are extremely productive, so we have many nesting species. Furthermore, migrants come from all points of the compass to spend time here, making our coast a highly desirable destination for birders. Open salt water is host to a great variety of water birds, from albatrosses to alcids, that feed at the surface or below it, some moving through the open water and others diving to the bottom to capture their prey. There are many vantage points to scan saltwater habitats, including Semiahmoo Spit, Point Wilson, Point No Point, Discovery Park, Point Defiance Park, Cape Flattery, Point Brown at Ocean Shores, Westport, and Cape Disappointment State Park. Try one of the many Washington State ferries, especially during winter.

2) ROCKY SHORE

Rocky shores are featured on exposed saltwater points and

beaches where mud and sand do not accumulate. A multitude of invertebrates live on and among the rocks on cobbled beaches, jetties, breakwaters, and rocky outcroppings. Alki Point, Deception Pass, Penn Cove, Olympic Peninsula coastal localities, and the jetties at Point Brown and Westport attract a selection of birds that prefer this habitat, including cormorants, Heermann's and other gulls, and Black Oystercatchers and other rock shorebirds, while Harlequin Ducks roost on the rocks and feed in the waters offshore. Most of the offshore islands in Washington, some with huge colonies of breeding seabirds, feature this habitat.

3) Sandy Shore, Mudflats, and Salt Marsh

Open ocean beaches are broad expanses of sand full of marine invertebrates, attractive to shorebirds and gulls. Sand beaches border the open ocean from Grays Harbor southward but recur throughout the protected waters of the Salish Sea. The substrate is finer in sheltered bays and estuaries, deposited as mud, and the mud has an even greater abundance and diversity of animals that furnish prey for birds. The extensive mudflats of Skagit Bay, Port Susan Bay, Deer Lagoon, the Nisqually National Wildlife Refuge, Dungeness Bay, Grays Harbor, and Willapa Bay offer feeding habitat for migrating and wintering shorebirds, while Padilla Bay's mudflats provide food for large numbers of wintering waterfowl. Salt marshes occur at the upper ends of estuaries and the protected sides of spits, where a variety of salt-tolerant plants such as Pickleweed can take root. These marshes host many ducks and shorebirds during migration and winter.

4) Fresh Water, Marsh, and Shore

Freshwater habitats provide an abundance of resources for

birds, both nesting sites free from predators and a great array of prey animals and plants. Mergansers, loons, grebes, Great Blue Herons, Bald Eagles, Ospreys, and Belted Kingfishers obtain fish from the open waters. Tennant Lake, Lake Washington, Lake Sammamish, Capitol Lake, and Vancouver Lake are just some of the many lakes with open water and bordering marshes that attract birds in the region. National wildlife refuges such as Nisqually and Ridgefield feature rich freshwater systems. Insects emerge in great numbers from these cattail and bulrush marshes, furnishing food for Virginia Rails, swallows, Marsh Wrens, and Red-winged Blackbirds.

5) WET CONIFEROUS FOREST

This habitat is the dominant vegetation of the region, with Douglas-fir, Western Hemlock, and Western Redcedar at low and middle elevations and Sitka Spruce and Shore Pine in coastal areas. Old-growth forests feature a diversity of tree heights and understory conditions, but logging has reduced many of the forests to uniform stands, typically of Douglas-fir. These forests are home to numerous species, including the endangered Spotted Owl and Marbled Murrelet and a great variety of passerine birds, including Olive-sided and Hammond's Flycatchers, Steller's Jays, Chestnut-backed Chickadees, Pacific Wrens, Golden-crowned Kinglets, Varied Thrushes, Western Tanagers, and Yellow-rumped Warblers. At higher elevations, for example at our main mountain passes, forests of Pacific Silver Fir, Mountain Hemlock, and Subalpine Fir host Sooty Grouse, Canada Jays, Hermit Thrushes, and Townsend's Warblers.

6) BROADLEAF FOREST

This habitat features stands of Red Alder, Black Cottonwood, Bigleaf and Vine Maple, and Pacific Madrone. Extensive broadleaf woodlands form a riparian zone along rivers and streams throughout the region—as in the Skagit, Stillaguamish, Snoqualmie, Nisqually, Dungeness, and Chehalis River valleys. Broadleaf trees also grow in mixed stands with conifers as well as in uniform stands during the early succession after logging or fires. Species of broadleaf forest include Ruffed Grouse, Downy Woodpeckers, Western Wood-Pewees, Pacific-slope Flycatchers, Hutton's and Warbling Vireos, Black-capped Chickadees, and Black-throated Gray Warblers. Willow Flycatchers, Red-eyed Vireos, and Yellow Warblers are common in riparian stands.

7) OAK PRAIRIES

This restricted lowland habitat occurs in some of the driest parts of the region, for example the San Juan Islands in the rain shadow of the Olympic Mountains and areas of well-drained soils in the Puget Sound lowlands. It is characterized by native grasslands and scattered stands of Garry Oak. The most extensive remaining examples are the South Sound Prairies that dot the fast-draining, gravelly soils extending from Joint Base Lewis-McChord west to Tenino and Littlerock. Scattered patches occur south of this to the Columbia River. Birds to be found in such places include California Quail, Common Nighthawks, House Wrens, Western Bluebirds, and Chipping Sparrows.

8) SUBALPINE PARKLAND AND ALPINE MEADOWS

This high-elevation, open habitat of the Cascades and Olympics consists of meadows with alpine wildflowers and scattered stands of trees. Look here for White-tailed Ptarmigan, Horned Lark, Mountain Bluebird, American Pipit, and Gray-crowned Rosy-Finch. Paradise and Sunrise at Mount Rainier National Park, Hurricane Ridge and Deer Park in Olympic

National Park, Mount Baker, and the North Cascades Highway offer good access to this habitat.

9) SHRUBBY THICKETS

Shrubby thickets are often present in clearings and around the edges of coniferous and broadleaf woods as well as powerline corridors. These thickets consist of a variety of shrubs, including willows, Twinberry Honeysuckle, Red-flowering Currant, Red-osier Dogwood, and huckleberries, some of which provide nectar for hummingbirds and fruits for thrushes and waxwings. Willow Flycatchers, Bushtits, Bewick's Wrens, Orange-crowned and MacGillivray's Warblers, Spotted Towhees, and Song and White-crowned Sparrows breed in this habitat anywhere in the lowlands.

10) PARKS AND GARDENS

This urban and suburban habitat varies greatly in the density and type of plantings, often incorporating native trees and shrubs that have been left in place or selectively planted, along with ornamental trees, shrubs, perennials and annual plants. Flowering herbs and shrubs provide nectar for humming-birds, and fruiting trees and shrubs attract a great variety of birds which benefit from not only the fruits but the insects attracted to them. Finally, bird feeders attract hummingbirds, woodpeckers, chickadees, nuthatches, grosbeaks, sparrows, juncos, and finches, as well as the Sharp-shinned and Cooper's Hawks that feed on them. This habitat of Parks and Gardens also hosts our most familiar birds—Rock Pigeons, American Crows, American Robins, European Starlings, and House Sparrows.

11) FARMLAND AND PASTURES

Farmlands and pastures, necessary for human life, also provide habitats for numerous bird species. When the fields where we harvest pumpkins and tulips, strawberries and corn, are fallow, they are sources of insect larvae and earthworms to flocks of shorebirds, gulls, crows, starlings, and blackbirds. Merlins and Peregrine Falcons are there to prey on these birds. The harvest leaves behind a rich mix of plant parts that Tundra and Trumpeter Swans, Snow, Canada, and Cackling Geese, and Sandhill Cranes find irresistible. In addition, overgrown farmland and pastures are perfect habitats for voles, which in turn attract Great Blue Herons, hawks and eagles, and ravens. Prime examples of farmlands are the Skagit, Samish, and Lummi Flats, the Snoqualmie Valley, and the Vancouver Lake bottoms.

Conservation

Increased development of the Puget Sound Region's urban and rural communities has led to changes in and loss of habitat, impacting our local bird populations. Pollution of Puget Sound waters by farms, pulp mills, sewage, marinas, garbage dumps, and storm runoff has had a direct effect on the region's waterbirds. Some populations have seen declines of up to 80 percent over the last 20 years. Deforestation has also taken its toll, as has urban and suburban sprawl. A diverse and thriving bird life is an excellent indicator of a healthy environment.

Those who enjoy birds should do all they can to protect birds and their habitats. We urge you to join one of the many conservation organizations such as local Audubon chapters, the Washington Wilderness Coalition, the Washington Environmental Council, or The Nature Conservancy of Washington that strive to address and improve environmental conditions.

Helpful Resources

There are a number of ways to get additional information about birds and their habitats, bird identification, and good places to go birding. Some of the best information is available through books, birding organizations, web sites, and local nature stores. Here are some of our favorites:

Eugene S. Hunn. 2012. *Birding in Seattle and King County*, 2nd ed. Seattle Audubon Society. Abundance, geographical distribution of birds; graphs of seasonal status; dozens of birding routes discussed, mapped.

The Great Washington State Birding Trail: Cascade Loop (2002), *Southwest Loop (2005), Olympic Loop (2007), and Puget Loop (2012)*. Olympia, Washington: Audubon Washington. Maps, descriptions of over 100 birding sites in the Puget Sound Region. Mobile app - Birding Trail WA available through website:
http://wa.audubon.org/great-washington-state-birding-trail

Mark G. Lewis and Fred A. Sharpe. 1987. *Birding in the San Juan Islands*. Seattle: The Mountaineers. Full accounts of species present in archipelago; when and where to find them.

Philip H. Zalesky. 2001. *Birding in Snohomish County*, rev. ed. Everett, Washington: Pilchuck Audubon Society. Good selection of birding sites, with maps.

Terence R. Wahl. 1995. *Birds of Whatcom County Status and Distribution*. Bellingham, Washington: The Author. Species accounts; valuable discussions of habitats, historical changes.

Terence R. Wahl, Bill Tweit, and Steven G. Mlodinow. 2005. *Birds of Washington: Status and Distribution*. Corvallis: Oregon State University Press. The most comprehensive treatment of the birds of our state.

Washington Ornithological Society. 2015. *A Birder's Guide to Washington, 2nd edition*. Includes hundreds of birding routes, over 220 maps, species accounts, status and habitat associations, seasonal abundance graphs.

IDENTIFICATION GUIDES

David Allen Sibley. 2003. *The Sibley Field Guide to Birds of Western North America*. New York: Alfred A. Knopf.

Jon L. Dunn and Jonathan Alderfer. *Field Guide to the Birds of North America,* Sixth Edition. 2011. Washington, D. C.: National Geographic Society.

Kenn Kaufman. 2005. *Kaufman Field Guide to Birds of North America*. New York: Houghton Mifflin.

Roger Tory Peterson. 2010. *Peterson Field Guide to Western Birds,* Fourth Edition. Boston: Houghton Mifflin Harcourt.

OTHER REGIONAL BIRDING RESOURCES

Seventeen local *Audubon Society* chapters exist throughout the Puget Sound Region. They provide an excellent means to learn more about birds. Most chapters have a newsletter, meetings, and local field trips to search for birds. Many have web sites with information about good places to go birding. Visit Audubon Washington at http://wa.audubon.org/audubon-locations and follow the chapter links.

BirdWeb (at www.birdweb.org), created by the Seattle Audubon Society, is an excellent resource for information on the birds of the Puget Sound Region.

Tweeters is an e-mail list on birds and birding sponsored by the Burke Museum at the University of Washington. Some 2,000 subscribers make Tweeters a lively forum and a good place to keep up with interesting bird sightings in the region. Visit the Tweeters web site at www.scn.org/tweeters/ for subscription instructions.

The *Washington Ornithological Society* (WOS), open to all persons interested in birds, offers monthly meetings in Seattle, field trips, a newsletter and other publications, and an annual conference. Visit the WOS web site at www.wos.org for information on membership and upcoming activities.

The Tweeters and Washington Ornithological Society web sites offer useful links to other birding resources.

NATURE STORES

Seattle Audubon Society Nature Shop, 8050 35th Avenue NE, Seattle, WA 98115 (phone 206-523-4483, www.seattleaudubon.org/sas/TheNatureShop.aspx) has a fine selection of books along with seed, bird feeders, and optics. A number of other local Audubon Society chapters also sell seed, bird feeders, and books.

There are a number of Wild Birds Unlimited stores in the region as well as other nature shops. Their staffs are always eager to answer your bird and bird-feeding questions. You can easily find these shops by searching online.

Species Accounts

The following pages present accounts and photographs of the most familiar bird species of the Puget Sound Region. Information on each species is presented in a standardized format: see the sample page (opposite) for an explanation. Species are grouped by families, color-coded and thumb-indexed. The Quick Guide on the first page inside the front cover of the book will help you locate the birds.

The following terms are used to describe the relative abundance of each species and the likelihood of finding it in a particular season. These definitions were developed by the American Birding Association.

- **Common:** Found in moderate to large numbers and easily found in appropriate habitat at the right time of year.
- **Fairly Common:** Found in small to moderate numbers and usually easy to find in appropriate habitat at the right time of year.
- **Uncommon:** Found in small numbers, and usually but not always found with some effort in appropriate habitat at the right time of year.
- **Rare:** Occurs annually in very small numbers. Not to be expected on any given day, but may be found with extended effort over the course of the appropriate season(s).

Birds shown in the photographs in the Species Accounts are adults unless the captions indicate otherwise.

NAME OF THE SPECIES
Scientific name

Description: Length (and wingspan for larger species), followed by a description that includes differences in plumages among sexes and ages. Key field marks, unique markings visible in the field that help distinguish one species from another, are shown in **boldfaced** type.

Similar Species: Identifies similar-appearing species and describes how to tell them apart.

Status and Habitat: Identifies the times of year during which the species is here and its relative abundance (see facing page for definitions of abundance terms). Also describes its habitat preferences and occurrence within the region.

Behavior: Identifies the prime sources of food and highlights behaviors characteristic of this species.

Voice: Describes the main song and calls of the species.

Did you know? Provides interesting facts about this species.

Date & Location Seen: A place for you to record the date and location of your first sighting of this species.

Juvenile

Adult

Description: 28", wingspan 53". **Large brown goose** with white belly, **pinkish-orange bill and orange legs**. ADULT: White patch around bill and black splotches on underparts. IMMATURE: lacks those markings. In flight, tail shows white basal ring and tip.

Similar Species: All other brown geese have black head and neck with white cheeks and throat or white necklace. Barnyard geese (domesticated from Old World Greylag Goose and Swan Goose) much like Greater White-fronted but have pink bill and legs, never white around bill or black speckles on underparts.

Status and Habitat: Common outer coastal migrant spring (April–May) and fall (September–October), especially Grays Harbor and Willapa Bay. Prefers estuaries, salt marshes, and open fields, less often freshwater lakes and ponds. Much less common through interior but might be seen anywhere; winters in very small numbers.

Behavior: Grazes on herbaceous vegetation in open areas. Often in large flocks overhead in migration. Wandering individuals usually in flocks of more common geese.

Voice: Typical goose, with high-pitched yelping *kah-la-luck*.

Did you know? Most North American geese are increasing, favored by our agricultural practices and creation of wildlife refuges. With larger numbers, some populations are overgrazing their breeding grounds.

Date & Location Seen: _____

_____

Juvenile

Adult

Description: 28", wingspan 54". White goose with **black wingtips**, pinkish legs, **pink bill with blackish "grinning patch."** IMMATURE: Dusky upperparts, grayish legs. Dark variant called Blue Goose (rare in region) blue-gray with white head and neck.

Similar Species: Swans larger, without black wingtips. Ross's Goose (not shown; rare in region) smaller with stubby bill. White domestic geese lack grinning patch and black wingtips.

Status and Habitat: Common but very local winter resident in short-grass or post-harvesting agricultural fields and estuaries; arrives October, departs by May. Local wintering grounds mostly limited to Skagit and Stillaguamish River deltas near Conway and Stanwood. Stragglers or California-bound migrants noted widely elsewhere in lowlands. Most birds wintering in region come from Wrangel Island, Siberia.

Behavior: Forages mostly on land but also in shallow water, almost entirely on plant materials including grasses, shoots, and waste grain. Highly gregarious. Noisy, single-species flocks can number in thousands, appear blizzard-like when flushed by marauding eagle.

Voice: Highly vocal. Raucous, high-pitched, honking yelps reach a crescendo when a flock lifts off.

Did you know? Snow Geese are often called "wavies" due to the undulating, irregular waves they form in flight.

Date & Location Seen: _____

Description: 24", wingspan 42". Stocky, short-necked, small-billed goose, **mostly blackish** with black bill and legs; white rump, undertail; barred whitish flanks; **white neck-ring**. All dark with white rear in flight. JUVENILE: Lacks neck ring in fall.

Similar Species: Cackling Goose and Canada Goose (page 31) with white chin patch; most races larger, with longer bill.

Status and Habitat: Common but local winter resident on protected bays and estuaries all along coast, rarely seen away from salt water; arrives November, departs by May. Good locations include Dungeness, Birch Bay, Padilla Bay. Numbers swelled by spring migrants, February–April, when common up and down Puget Sound.

Behavior: Forages by grazing on tidal flats and wading and upending in shallow water. Diet primarily two species of leafy marine plants, eelgrass and sea lettuce; birds feed in open water when these plants are floating in tidelines. Highly gregarious but rarely flocks with other species, although sometimes single birds in flocks of other geese away from the coast. Flies low over ocean in ragged lines.

Voice: Quietly murmured, nasal *rrok rrok*.

Did you know? Most West Coast Brants come from Alaska, have dark bellies. Birds from a central Arctic population wintering in Padilla Bay have gray bellies.

Date & Location Seen: _____

Canada Goose

Cackling Goose

Description: Variable. Smallest **Cackling** 22″, wingspan 43″; largest **Canada** 43″, wingspan 60″. Range from light to dark brown with black legs, bill, and tail; white rump and undertail; **black head, neck with white chin patch. Cackling** with shorter neck, smaller bill.

Similar Species: Brant (page 29) lacks white chin patch. Greater White-fronted Goose (page 25) has brown neck, orange bill and legs.

Status and Habitat: Cackling common migrant and winter resident, mostly on and near coast. More common to south but recently increasing northward. **Canada** common and widespread throughout lowlands, with resident large race and migrant smaller ones. Less common but occurs inland at higher elevations. Migratory races of both arrive October, depart by May, common on ponds, lakes, marshes, grassy fields, estuaries, slow rivers.

Behavior: Forage mostly on land but also in water, primarily for plant materials. **Canada** did not formerly breed in region, but introduced populations habituated to humans now thrive year-round in urban areas.

Voice: Typical goose honk; smaller races of **Cackling** higher-pitched yelping.

Did you know? Three races of Cackling Goose and four of Canada Goose occur in the region. Large races of Cackling and small of Canada can be difficult to separate. Canada often hybridizes with domestic geese.

Date & Location Seen: _____

Trumpeter Swan

Tundra Swan

Description: 60" / 52", wingspan 80" / 66". **Huge, white, long-necked** waterfowl with bill black in adult, pinkish in juvenile. **Trumpeter** Larger; long **black bill extends to eye in broad triangle**; juvenile retains gray plumage through spring. **Tundra** Smaller; **black of bill constricted at eye**; usually yellow mark before eye; **juvenile white by spring.**

Similar Species: Snow Goose (page 27) smaller, has black wing-tips. Introduced Mute Swan (not shown) has orange bill with black knob at base.

Status and Habitat: Common winter residents (early November–March), primarily northern portion of region; **Tundra** also along Lower Columbia River, Ridgefield Refuge. Both use lakes, ponds, marshes, coastal bays, and agricultural fields. **Trumpeter** more tied to fresh water than **Tundra** and more likely on small water bodies.

Behavior: Forage on plant materials on land or in water, including waste grains, potatoes. Gregarious, often in flocks including both species; may roost on open water.

Voice: Trumpeter lower-pitched single notes, like trumpet. **Tundra** gooselike barking *klow wow*.

Did you know? The Trumpeter Swan, close to extinction a century ago, is rapidly recovering. Birds wintering in Washington come from populations that nest in Alaska. Reintroduced widely in North America.

Date & Location Seen: _____

Male

Female

Description: 17", wingspan 30". Unique, short-necked duck with long, broad tail, **swept-back crest**, dark blue speculum bordered at rear by white, iridescent blue wingtips. MALE: Spectacularly **rainbow-colored**. Mostly green head with vivid white lines; scarlet eye and bill base. Dull in summer, retaining head pattern, red bill. FEMALE: Brown with white-spotted sides and broad **teardrop-shaped eye-ring**.

Similar Species: None; vaguely similar Mandarin Duck (native to eastern Asia) rarely escapes from captivity.

Status and Habitat: Fairly common summer resident in lowlands to moderate elevations at wooded swamps and ponds and shady, slow rivers; sometimes on city park lakes. Uncommon and local in winter (beginning October); migrants return March.

Behavior: Forages mostly by picking in water, seldom upending. Diet mainly seeds; takes more insects and other animal prey in summer. Nests in cavities. Often perches on large tree branches. Disperses late summer–fall, may gather in small groups outside nesting season.

Voice: Male gives thin, high whistles, female penetrating *oooeeek* when flushed or alarmed.

Did you know? Threatened with extinction a century ago by overhunting, Wood Ducks have recovered, aided in part by placement of thousands of nest boxes.

Date & Location Seen: _____

Male

Female

Description: 19″, wingspan 33″. Medium-sized, rather plain dabbling duck with white belly, puffy head, yellow feet, **white speculum**. MALE: Mostly plain, finely barred gray with rusty back plumes, black bill, **black rump and undertail**; dull as female in summer. FEMALE: Mottled brown with yellowish-orange sides of bill.

Similar Species: Female Mallard (page 41) bulkier, more patterned head, lacks white speculum.

Status and Habitat: Common year-round resident throughout lowlands in ponds, lakes, marshes. Some movement to salt water habitats such as estuaries in winter but prefers fresh water. Next to Mallard, most common breeding duck.

Behavior: Forages primarily for plant material; dabbles at surface, upends, or occasionally grazes on land. Usually small flocks, often with other dabblers. Steals water plants from coots that dive and bring them up. Pair formation begins by fall.

Voice: Male with low-pitched *reb reb* call, also squeaky whistle during courtship. Female gives nasal quack, softer than that of Mallard.

Did you know? Gadwalls were historically present in much lower numbers in the Puget Sound Region. Their dramatic increase in recent times is probably due to the spread of Eurasian watermilfoil, an invasive water plant that is a favored food.

Date & Location Seen: _____

American Wigeon
Male

Female

Eurasian Wigeon
Male

Female

Description: 19″, wingspan 32″. Puffy-headed dabbling ducks with small bluish bill, relatively long tail, **white forewing patch**. MALES: **American** with **brownish sides, gray head,** white forehead, green behind eye. **Eurasian** with **gray sides, reddish head,** yellowish forehead. FEMALES: **American** with light brown head contrasting with reddish sides. **Eurasian** all reddish brown.

Similar Species: Gadwall (page 37) has white in speculum, not forewing; female has yellow on bill.

Status and Habitat: American common winter resident, widespread in lowlands on ponds, marshes, estuaries, bays, and open fields; arrives late August, departs by May; very rare breeder on ponds. **Eurasian** uncommon winter resident in same habitats, usually in flocks of Americans; arrives later in fall. Eurasians usually easy to find at Samish Flats, Dungeness; often one or two in American Wigeon flocks at city parks, e.g., Green Lake (Seattle), Point Defiance Park (Tacoma).

Behavior: Mostly plant material. Graze on land much more than other ducks. Forage in water by skimming surface, rarely upending; also steal plants from coots and diving ducks. Form large, tight flocks, especially on land.

Voice: Distinctive *wee whee whir* whistled by male **American**; female with growling quack. Male **Eurasian** has single loud whistle.

Did you know? Small bills of wigeons are like those of geese, perfect for grazing.

Date & Location Seen: _____

Male

Female

Description: 22", wingspan 35". Large, **heavy-bodied** dabbling duck with orange legs, **blue speculum** bordered white fore and aft. MALE: Grayish sides with darker back, **chestnut breast, white neck-ring**, yellow bill, **iridescent green head**, curled-up central tail feathers; in summer dull as female. FEMALE: Mottled brown with orange and black bill.

Similar Species: Female Gadwall (page 37) less bulky, plainer puffier head, white speculum. No other dabbler has blue and white speculum (not always visible).

Status and Habitat: Common breeder throughout lowlands in ponds, lakes, and marshes, numbers augmented in winter when they also occupy estuaries, flooded fields, and agricultural lands. Found in every city park with a lake.

Behavior: Forages for plant and animal matter by dabbling, upending, or grazing on land. Sociable, often flocking with other dabblers. Pair formation begins by fall, courtship behavior easy to see. Tame in urban areas, providing lessons in duck behavior.

Voice: Male with low-pitched *reeb reeb* call, also grunt and squeaky whistle when courting. Female gives characteristic nasal, irritating quack.

Did you know? Mallards were first domesticated in Asia thousands of years ago and now occur in a bewildering variety of breeds; an unknown duck in a city park may well be one of them.

Date & Location Seen: _____

_____

Blue-winged Teal
Male

Female

Cinnamon Teal
Male

Female

Description: 15", wingspan 23". Small dabblers with long, dark bill, green speculum, **powder-blue forewing patch** visible in flight. **Blue-winged:** MALE brown spotted with black with white flank patch, head gray with **bold white crescent behind bill**; dull as female in summer. FEMALE mottled brown with pale area behind bill. **Cinnamon:** MALE **chestnut-red** with red eye; dull as female in summer. FEMALE mottled brown with plain face, dark brown eye. Difficult to distinguish female Blue-winged from Cinnamon but latter has longer bill, lacks pale area on face. All birds of these species dull in late summer/fall, unidentifiable at distance.

Similar Species: Green-winged Teal (page 49) smaller, shorter-billed, lacks blue forewing patch.

Status and Habitat: **Blue-winged** uncommon breeder in ponds and marshes, favoring smaller water bodies; much more common as late May and early fall migrant. **Cinnamon** fairly common breeder, present from April through September, when small flocks migrate through; rare in winter. Both can be at marine estuaries in fall.

Behavior: Both species forage for plant and animal matter in shallows, rarely upending. **Blue-winged** eats more insects. Fast, agile fliers, often in small mixed groups of teals.

Voice: Females quack; males chatter and whistle.

Did you know? Closely related Blue-winged and Cinnamon Teals hybridize rarely but regularly.

Date & Location Seen: _____

Male

Female

Description: 18", wingspan 29". Fairly small dabbling duck with **large spoon-shaped bill**, green speculum, **powder-blue forewing patch visible in flight**, orange legs. MALE: White breast, **rust-brown belly and sides**; iridescent green head, yellow eye, black bill. Dull as female in summer. FEMALE: Mottled brown with dark eye, orange bill.

Similar Species: Bill size and shape distinctive. Wing pattern identical to Blue-winged and Cinnamon Teal (page 43).

Status and Habitat: Common winter resident August–May, widespread in lowland ponds, lakes, marshes, estuaries, and flooded fields. Particularly common at sewage lagoons. Uncommon breeder in marshy ponds.

Behavior: Forages while swimming by sweeping bill from side to side to filter surface water for tiny plants and animals. Circling behavior of single birds, pairs, and even large, tight groups draws microorganisms up in water column. Single-species flocks because of this feeding behavior. Courting and pair formation begin late winter; male attains breeding plumage later than other dabblers.

Voice: Male gives low calls during courtship; female quacks hoarsely.

Did you know? Shoveler filter-feeding is not so different from that of baleen whales. The greatly enlarged lamellae on the edges of the mandibles act as sieves, trapping food particles as water is expelled from the bill.

Date & Location Seen: _____

Male

Female

Description: 20″ (male 26″ with tail), wingspan 33″. **Slender**, long-necked dabbling duck with long, narrow bill, **green to violet speculum** bordered with buff at front, white at rear. MALE: Grayish with long, needle-like tail, dark brown head, **white on breast extending in thin line up side of neck, blue-gray bill**; dull as female in summer. FEMALE: Mottled grayish brown with short, pointed tail, **unmarked head, dark-gray bill**.

Similar Species: Slender shape, unmarked head and dark bill separate female pintail from other dabblers.

Status and Habitat: Common winter resident at ponds, marshes, estuaries, shallow lakes, and flooded fields in lowlands. Less likely to be found in urbanized areas than other dabblers. Rare breeder in marshy ponds. Highly migratory, with transients arriving by August, departing by May.

Behavior: Mostly tips up in shallow water, also walks on land or mudflats to forage. Diet mainly plant material, including waste grain, also takes aquatic invertebrates. Sometimes in very large groups, often with other dabblers. Courting and pair formation begin in winter.

Voice: Fairly vocal, male with fluty *toop toop*, also high wheezy calls; female *kuk-kuk-kuk*.

Did you know? Northern Pintail is usually the most abundant duck in the Pacific flyway, although numbers fluctuate greatly, as the species is much affected by drought on breeding grounds.

Date & Location Seen: _____

Male

Male

Female

GREEN-WINGED TEAL
Anas crecca

Description: 13", wingspan 23". **Small** dabbling duck with **short, dark bill, green speculum**. MALE: Grayish with chestnut-and-green head, cream undertail, **white vertical bar on side**; dull as female in summer. FEMALE: Mottled brown with dark line through eye, white line around undertail.

Similar Species: Smaller, more compact, shorter-billed than other dabblers; female eye-line more pronounced and usually dusky mark on cheek as well.

Status and Habitat: Common winter resident in lowland ponds, marshes, estuaries, bays, shallow lakes, and flooded fields. Rare breeder at marshy ponds and sewage lagoons. Highly migratory, with transients arriving by August, departing by May.

Behavior: Forages by dabbling in shallow water or while walking on wet mud, filtering water and mud for plant seeds and invertebrates. Gathers in large or small groups, often with other ducks. Flocks fly swiftly in tight units, leaving water quickly, with little effort. Courting and pair formation begin in winter.

Voice: Male highly vocal with ringing *peep*; female gives weak, nasal quack.

Did you know? The Eurasian race, called Common Teal, is a rare winter visitor. It features a white line along each side instead of a vertical white bar.

Date & Location Seen: _____

Male

Female

Description: 21", wingspan 29". Sleek, elegant, long-necked diving duck with **sloping forehead, long, dark bill**, plain grayish wings with slightly paler wing stripe. MALE: Black at both ends with **snowy white back and sides. Head and neck chestnut-reddish**; eye red. FEMALE: Light brown overall with dark eye.

Similar Species: Distinctive head shape and plumage separate Canvasback from scaups (page 57). Male Redhead (page 53) distinguished by differently shaped head and bill, paler red head, gray back.

Status and Habitat: Fairly common but local winter resident throughout lowlands on lakes, estuaries, coastal bays, and sewage ponds; arrives by October, most depart by April. Good locations include Drayton Harbor, Everett sewage lagoons.

Behavior: Dives, mostly in shallow water, primarily for plants, including tubers in bottom mud. Gathers in flocks, often with scaups and Redheads. Flight very rapid and, as in other diving ducks, wing-beat more rapid than in dabbling ducks because wings smaller. Most pair formation occurs in spring on migration.

Voice: Grunts from female and cooing sounds from male seldom heard on wintering grounds.

Did you know? The Canvasback's species name, *valisineria*, refers to wild celery (*Vallisneria*)—an important food item.

Date & Location Seen: _____

Male

Female

Description: 19", wingspan 29". Medium-sized **round-headed** diving duck with black-tipped, blue-gray bill. MALE: **Gray with red head, black breast** and rear. FEMALE: **Light to medium brown** all over, bill duller.

Similar Species: Combination of head shape and color and body color distinguishes from Canvasback (page 51). Female like Ring-necked Duck (page 55) but with rounder, paler head and no prominent ring on bill.

Status and Habitat: Uncommon and local in lowlands on lakes and large ponds, sewage ponds, and slow-floating rivers, mostly in fall migration (mostly November); much smaller numbers winter, very few in spring (mostly April). Large lakes best, including Lake Washington in Seattle and Everett and Hoquiam sewage lagoons.

Behavior: Dives for food, both plants and animals in migration. Usually in flocks with Canvasback, scaups.

Voice: Male has wheezy *whee-ou* call, almost like cat meow, most often heard during courtship in late winter and spring. Female gives soft, repeated *err* sounds.

Did you know? Redheads are brood parasites, many females laying a few eggs in the nests of other ducks, both their own and other species. If the female's nest is destroyed, she may still have surviving offspring.

Date & Location Seen: _____

Male

Female

Description: 17", wingspan 24". Short-necked diving duck with **peaked head, white ring near tip of gray bill**, grayish wing stripes in flight. MALE: Purplish iridescent head, **black back** and breast; **vertical white mark on gray side** in front of wing. FEMALE: Brown with **white eye-ring**, diffuse pale area near bill.

Similar Species: Lesser Scaup (page 57) head less peaked, no ring on bill, male with gray back, female with bold white face patch at bill base. Redhead (page 53) female a bit larger and paler, round head, only faint hint of pale bill ring.

Status and Habitat: Common winter resident on wooded ponds, lakes, sewage lagoons; prefers fresh water. Arrives by September, most depart by May. Also rare breeder on forested lakes in lowlands; has nested in San Juan and Thurston Counties.

Behavior: Mostly dives to feed on aquatic plants and insects but may also dabble in fairly shallow water. Flocks may be large or small, single-species or mixed with other divers on large water bodies; also flocks with dabblers on small ponds.

Voice: Male whistles, female growls softly.

Did you know? Unlike other diving ducks, Ring-necked Ducks are able to spring directly off the water into flight, enabling them to use small ponds surrounded by trees.

Date & Location Seen: _____

Greater Scaup

Female

Lesser Scaup

Female

Description: 18" / 17", wingspan 28" / 26". Short-necked diving ducks with bluish-gray bills, **white wing stripes** visible in flight. MALES: **Black at both ends, whitish in middle**, head darkly iridescent. FEMALES: Brown with **white facial patch at bill base**. **Greater** with **round head**, bill wider, male's head glossed greenish. **Lesser** with **peaked crown**, bill smaller, male's head glossed purplish, wing stripe extends only halfway to wingtip. Head shape distinguishes females but altered while diving.

Similar Species: Ring-necked Duck (page 55) head more peaked, pale ring near bill tip; male with black back, vertical white mark on side. Male goldeneyes (page 71) with much black on backs. Other brown females have different head markings.

Status and Habitat: Common winter residents at lakes, sewage lagoons, bays and estuaries. **Greater** much more common on salt water, **Lesser** on fresh water. Both arrive by October, depart in May. Lesser also rare breeder at lowland sewage ponds.

Behavior: Dive for variety of aquatic animals and plants. **Greater** often dabbles near shore. Commonly gather in tighter flocks than other ducks, may include both scaup species and other close relatives.

Voice: Grating sounds, deep whistles.

Did you know? Iridescence is a tricky thing; each species can at times show the iridescent color of the other.

Date & Location Seen: _____

Male

Female

Description: 16″, wingspan 26″. Compact, round-headed diving duck with **steep forehead, tiny bill**. MALE: Darkly colored, mostly **slate-blue with rusty sides, bold white marks** on head, sides, and back; more like female in summer. FEMALE: Brown with white spots on head.

Similar Species: Female scoters (pages 63-67) much heavier with larger bills, sloping foreheads. Female Bufflehead (page 69) smaller with white wing patch, only one white patch on face.

Status and Habitat: Fairly common winter visitor on rocky coast, both bays and exposed locations. Good locations include Semiahmoo Spit, Ediz Hook, west side of Whidbey Island. Most birds leave in spring, some to breed on swift rocky streams in Cascades and Olympics. After females on nests, males come quickly back to coast, only absent during late spring. Breeders rarely observed but Skykomish, Snoqualmie and Dungeness Rivers worth checking.

Behavior: Forages mostly by diving for wide variety of marine invertebrates, insects while in fresh water; also picks from rocks at surface. In small flocks. Courtship begins in winter, pairs form in spring, move up rivers to nest.

Voice: Male has piercing whistle, female nasal quacks.

Did you know? Female Harlequin Ducks may share in the care of mixed broods.

Date & Location Seen: _____

Nonbreeding Male

Female

Breeding Male

Description: 16" (male 21" with tail), wingspan 28". Short-necked, white-bellied, **stubby-billed** diving duck, with entirely **blackish wings**. Very different breeding and nonbreeding plumages notable. MALE: Elegant, usually with **long, pointed tail**; bill dark with pink band. Breeding (spring–summer) plumage mostly brown and black with white face, non-breeding (fall–winter) **mostly white** with black wings, breast, and neck patch. FEMALE: Bill bluish-green; dark overall, much white on head and neck.

Similar Species: In flight, combination of dark wings and whitish body of nonbreeding male unique among ducks. Markings very different from equally long-tailed Northern Pintail (page 47), neck longer than black and white alcids (pages 201–205).

Status and Habitat: Locally fairly common winter resident in protected coastal waters; arrives mid October, departs by May. Rare in southern part of region; look for it especially in north (Point Roberts, Drayton Harbor) and west (Sequim Bay).

Behavior: Usually forages well offshore in deeper water than other diving ducks. Partially opens wings and dives deep for variety of marine invertebrates, uses wings rather than feet to move underwater. Usually in small flocks.

Voice: Male very vocal with loud *ow-owtaluk* when spring courtship begins in winter quarters. Female gives soft grunts.

Did you know? Accomplished divers, Long-tailed Ducks have been recorded at depths exceeding 200 feet.

Date & Location Seen: _____

Male

Female

Description: 20", wingspan 30". **Stocky** diving duck with broad, **bulging bill, sloping forehead.** MALE: All black with big **multicolored bill, white patches on head**, white eye. FEMALE: Dark eye, brown with two whitish patches on side of head, one on back. JUVENILE: Pale belly; male duller than adult and with dark eye; female lacks hindneck patch.

Similar Species: Black Scoter (page 67) female has entire lower face pale, male without white on head, although immature Surf Scoter may also lack white. White-winged Scoter (page 65) has white speculum and feathered bill base; bill meets head feathering in vertical line in Surf.

Status and Habitat: Common winter resident on coastal bays and estuaries, also open outer coast; most arrive by September, depart in May. Most common scoter, one of most common sea ducks.

Behavior: Forages by diving, almost exclusively for bivalves while in winter quarters. Dives by jumping forward with partially opened wings. Often flocks with other scoters and scaups. Pairs form during winter and spring. Male courtship involves flying low over water and splashing down with raised wings. Wings of male whistle in flight.

Voice: Male whistles, female utters croaking grunts.

Did you know? In heavy surf, Surf Scoters synchronize their dives with breaking waves, diving just before the crash.

Date & Location Seen: _____

Male

Male

Female

Description: 22", wingspan 33". **Large, heavy-billed** diving duck; **white speculum** visible while flying and diving but may be hidden when at rest. MALE: All black with white eye, small **white mark behind eye, reddish bill** with small black knob at base. FEMALE: Entirely dark brown with dark eye. JUVENILE: Dark brown with two white patches on either side of head, pale belly.

Similar Species: Other scoters (pages 63, 67) smaller, lack white speculum; Surf Scoter lacks feathering on bill base. Pigeon Guillemot (page 201) much smaller with weak flight, white patch at front of wing.

Status and Habitat: Common winter resident on coastal bays and estuaries, although less so than Surf. Most arrive by October, depart in May. Prefer large sandy bays.

Behavior: Dives with partially opened wings for variety of marine organisms, preference for clams (not mussels like other scoters). Often flocks with other scoters. Pairs form on winter quarters, courtship not as impressive as other scoters. Appears heavy in flight. Flocks move in long, wavering lines low over water. No wing whistling in this species.

Voice: Male whistles; female grunts seldom heard.

Did you know? Many birds change habitat drastically between seasons; this species breeds on cattail-bordered lakes.

Date & Location Seen: _____

Male

Female

Description: 19", wingspan 28". **Stocky** diving duck with **fairly small black bill**. MALE: All black with **yellow-orange knob** at bill base. FEMALE: Dark brown with **entire lower face and foreneck tan**. JUVENILE: Similar to female, with pale belly.

Similar Species: Bill much smaller than that of other scoters (pages 63–65), normal duck bill held more horizontal. Female with more extensive cheek patch (other female scoters have two or three small whitish patches). White-winged has white speculum. Ruddy Duck (page 79) male head pattern like female scoter but much smaller bird with large, broad bill, longer tail.

Status and Habitat: Locally fairly common winter resident on protected marine waters, usually with rocky bottom. Good bets include Drayton Harbor, Whidbey Island, Alki Point in Seattle. Arrives by November, departs by April.

Behavior: Diet primarily bivalves, obtained by diving; also takes other marine organisms. Often flocks with other scoters, even in tight groups. Courtship progresses throughout winter to spring. Wings of male whistle in flight.

Voice: More vocal than other scoters: male's mournful descending whistle characteristic.

Did you know? Black is the least common scoter in the region. Over 100,000 breed in Alaska, yet fewer than 5,000 winter on the Pacific Coast south of Anchorage.

Date & Location Seen: _____

Male

Female

Description: 13", wingspan 20". **Small**, plump diving duck, with **small gray bill**, white belly, **big white wing patches** (smaller in female). MALE: Mostly white with dark back, purple-green iridescent **puffy head with white patch at back**. FEMALE: Brown, light on sides, with **small, oval white cheek patch**.

Similar Species: Goldeneyes (page 71) larger, white patch of male in front of rather than behind eye. Hooded Merganser (page 73) male has rusty sides with black-and-white bars. Ruddy Duck (page 79) has larger bill, cheek patch.

Status and Habitat: Common winter resident on freshwater and saltwater habitats of all types and sizes in lowlands, very adaptable and one of most ubiquitous ducks. Can be in ponds barely large enough to be able to take off with a run. Most arrive October, depart by May.

Behavior: Dives for insects and other aquatic invertebrates. Usually in small groups, but large concentrations occur at favorable sites. Patters on surface with rapid wing-beats before flying. Male courtship in spring vigorous, incessant.

Voice: Fairly quiet in winter quarters but soft, growling whistles, grunts occasionally given.

Did you know? *Bucephala* comes from Greek meaning bull-headed. The species' English name evokes the high, domed forehead of the American bison (buffalo).

Date & Location Seen: _____

Common Goldeneye

Female

Barrow's Goldeneye

Female

Description: 18", wingspan 27". Plump, short-necked, with short bill, **puffy head**, big white wing patch (smaller in females). **Common** head peaked in middle. **Barrow's** head peaked at front, **steep forehead**, bill smaller. MALES: White with black-and-white back, dark iridescent head, white patch before eye. **Common** head green-black with **round white patch**; less black on back. **Barrow's** head purplish-black, **patch crescent-shaped**; more black on back. FEMALES: Grayish with brown head. **Barrow's** female with **orange bill** during winter, darkens in spring.

Similar Species: Bufflehead (page 69) smaller, male's white head patch behind rather than in front of eye.

Status and Habitat: Fairly common winter residents, arriving by November, departing by April. **Common** ubiquitous on protected salt water, locally common on freshwater lakes. **Barrow's** primarily on salt water, especially attracted to dock pilings. Barrow's breeds locally on forested mountain lakes.

Behavior: Dive for aquatic invertebrates of all kinds, **Barrow's** especially fond of mussels growing on pilings. Both form loose flocks outside nesting season, larger in Barrow's. Nest in tree cavities. Vigorous courtship in both species, displayed soon after fall arrival, includes throwing head back onto back.

Voice: Soft grunts.

Did you know? Male goldeneyes' wings create a loud whistling sound in flight. Females sometimes lay their eggs in the nests of other ducks.

Date & Location Seen: _____

Male

Female

Description: 16", wingspan 23". Small, **long-tailed** duck with thin, **saw-toothed bill**, conspicuous **puffy crest**, white belly. Small white wing patches visible in flight. MALE: Striking; mostly blackish above including bill, with **fan-shaped white crest** that can be raised and lowered, **rusty sides**, black-and-white side bars, ornamental back plumes; dull as female in late summer. FEMALE: Gray-brown with more reddish crest, yellowish-edged bill. Look like darts in flight.

Similar Species: Other mergansers (pages 75–77) larger, with reddish bills, large wing patches in males. Bufflehead (page 69) female smaller with short bill, small cheek patch; male has white sides.

Status and Habitat: Fairly common breeder at wooded freshwater ponds, sloughs, and sluggish creeks with emergent vegetation in lowlands. Migrants augment numbers in winter, when birds can also be found on sewage ponds and in protected marine waters.

Behavior: Forages by diving and swimming underwater for fish, aquatic insects, and crayfish. Usually in pairs or small groups. Often allows close approach, then patters along surface with rapid wing-beats, flies off. Nests in tree cavities, also nest boxes.

Voice: Fairly vocal with soft croaks.

Did you know? Hooded Mergansers occasionally hybridize with other cavity-nesting ducks, especially goldeneyes. Waterfowl hybridize more than other birds.

Date & Location Seen: _____

Male

Female

COMMON MERGANSER
Mergus merganser

Description: 24", wingspan 34". **Robust**, white-bellied diving duck, with thin, **reddish saw-toothed bill**. Large white wing patches (smaller in female) visible in flight. MALE: Body **mostly white** with dark green head, black back; dull as female in late summer. FEMALE: Gray with rich brown head, white chin.

Similar Species: Red-breasted Merganser (page 77) female very similar but less bulky, with neither distinct white throat nor abrupt line between light gray body and brown head; bill thinner at base. Hooded Merganser (page 73) much smaller, bill not reddish.

Status and Habitat: Common resident from lowlands to mountain passes. Breeds on clearwater forested rivers and lakes, families move downstream to brackish river mouths in late summer. Winters largely on fresh water but also in deep saltwater channels.

Behavior: Forages by diving and swimming underwater, sometimes long distances, for fish, including sculpins and salmonids; young eat aquatic insects. Concentrates in large flocks from late summer to early winter in rivers and estuaries where pair formation begins. Nests near water in tree cavities, mostly along rivers but also near clear lakes; may be loosely colonial.

Voice: Hoarse croaking notes.

Did you know? Males develop a peachy tone to the underparts in fall that eventually fades. In the Old World this species is called Goosander.

Date & Location Seen: _____

Male

Female

RED-BREASTED MERGANSER
Mergus serrator

Description: 22", wingspan 30". **Slim**, long-necked, white-bellied diving duck with long, thin, **reddish saw-toothed bill**, conspicuous **shaggy crest**. Large **white wing patches** (smaller in female) visible in flight. MALE: Elegant with green-black head, white neck ring, reddish breast, black back, gray sides. FEMALE: Gray-brown with reddish head. Mergansers look like javelins in flight.

Similar Species: Common Merganser (page 75) female very similar but larger, with dark red-brown head and distinct white throat contrasting with light gray body; bill thicker at base. Hooded Merganser (page 73) smaller, browner, bill not reddish.

Status and Habitat: Common winter resident on marine waters, both open channels and protected bays and estuaries. Most arrive October, depart by April. Occasional in migration and winter on large lakes.

Behavior: Forages by diving and swimming underwater for fish. Often submerges head to search. Loose flocks, sometimes dozens of birds, may fish cooperatively by herding schooling fish. Male's spectacular courtship behavior (featuring wide-open bill) increases through late fall and winter.

Voice: Relatively silent. Females may give harsh, grating squawks.

Did you know? One of the fastest-flying ducks, Red-breasted Mergansers have been clocked at 100 miles per hour.

Date & Location Seen: _____

Male

Nonbreeding Male

Female

Description: 15", wingspan 19". Compact, **large-headed, broad-billed** diving duck with **long, stiff tail** often cocked upward. MALE: In breeding plumage (spring–summer) rich rufous with black head and neck, **white cheek, powder-blue bill**; dull brown in fall–winter with same black cap and white cheek. FEMALE: Brownish, **light cheek crossed by dark line**.

Similar Species: Quite distinctive, only Cinnamon Teal (page 43) similarly colored. Female Black Scoter (page 67) only duck with head pattern similar to male's.

Status and Habitat: Locally common winter resident September–May on lakes, sewage lagoons, and protected bays. Uncommon breeder on lowland lakes with marshy edge.

Behavior: Dives, feeds on tiny animals and seeds by grubbing in bottom mud. Often in large groups in winter, most birds sleeping (food easily acquired). Poor flier with small wings; patters along water, flapping rapidly to take flight; clumsy on land. Male display remarkable—raises tail to expose white under it, pumps head rapidly, followed by "motor-boat" rushes across water.

Voice: Courting male produces stuttering series of ticks while pumping bill against inflated throat; female gives nasal call in defense of young.

Did you know? Unlike other ducks, Ruddies are dull in winter and molt to bright plumage in spring and summer, with courtship on their breeding grounds.

Date & Location Seen: _____

California Quail
Male

California Quail
Female

Mountain Quail

Description: 9". Elegantly plumaged, with **forward-drooping topknot. Grayish overall, scaled belly,** brown sides with white stripes. MALE: Chestnut patch on belly, **black face and throat outlined in white. Similar Species**: Mountain Quail (below) has long, upright head plume, plain belly, chestnut throat. **Status and Habitat:** Fairly common resident in lowlands, most numerous in more open and shrubby areas such as Sequim–Dungeness, San Juans, and South Sound Prairies. Introduced from California. **Behavior**: Eats plant material (mostly seeds) and some invertebrates. Collects in flocks in winter. Prolific, up to 20 eggs per clutch. **Voice**: Loud *chi ca go* assembly call; *pit pit pit* contact call. **Did you know?** Coveys post male sentries on prominent perches to warn of danger.

Description: 10". **Colorful quail with long, straight topknot**. Blue-gray with brown back, chestnut throat and flanks, latter heavily barred white. **Similar Species**: A bit larger than California Quail (above), which has scaled underparts and different head plume. **Status and Habitat**: Uncommon and local resident in early second growth south and west of Puget Sound in Kitsap, Thurston, and Grays Harbor counties. **Behavior**: Very skulking, pairs and small flocks move out from dense shrubbery to feed in open, then scurry back under cover when disturbed. Feeds on seeds and leaves on and near ground. **Voice**: Male utters clear two-noted whistle *quee-ark*. **Did you know?** Introduced to our region, native east of Cascades in Klickitat County and Blue Mountains.

Date & Location Seen: _____

Male

Female

Description: Male 28" female 19". Large **chickenlike** bird with **long tail**. Mostly mottled shades of brown. MALE: Very colorful, heavily patterned except for gray rump; **white neck ring, iridescent green head**, and **red wattles**. FEMALE: Light brown with dark bars and chevrons.

Similar Species: Other large "chickens" in lowlands, Ruffed and Sooty Grouse (page 85), have shorter, rounded tails and are darker than female pheasant; usually found in forests.

Status and Habitat: Uncommon year-round resident with patchy distribution throughout lowlands, e.g., Kitsap Peninsula, Sequim–Dungeness, Kent Valley. Pen-raised birds released for hunting help sustain naturalized populations. Prefers open fields, brush patches, woodland edges, lightly developed residential areas, and large parks.

Behavior: Forages mostly on ground, in or out of brush. Consumes agricultural grains, weed seeds, roots, fruits, nuts, leaves, insects, earthworms, and snails. Prefers to walk or run but strong flyer when flushed. Takes off explosively on whirring wings. Young follow female, forage for themselves upon hatching. May form flocks in winter.

Voice: Male crowing a loud, grating *koork-kok*; also softer clucking sounds by both sexes.

Did you know? Native to Asia but widely introduced as a game bird. The first successful introduction of pheasants to the United States was in Oregon's Willamette Valley in 1882, followed by Washington in 1883.

Date & Location Seen: _____

Ruffed Grouse

Sooty Groose
Male

Description: 16". Variably brownish, cryptically patterned, **chickenlike** bird with barred flanks, small crest. Either reddish or grayish, **tail with black band at tip. Similar Species**: Sooty Grouse (below) somewhat larger, tail dark with gray tip, male uniformly darker; inhabits conifer forests. **Status and Habitat**: Year-round resident in low to mid-elevation deciduous or mixed forest away from civilization, often along stream corridors. **Behavior**: Browses on leaves; buds important in winter. Chicks can fly within a week. Mostly solitary. Males "drum" from log and other ground perches in spring. **Voice**: Female sometimes makes clucking, cooing sounds. **Did you know?** Drumming is an accelerating series of sonic booms as air rushes to fill the vacuum produced by the male's wing movements.

SOOTY GROUSE *Dendragapus fuliginosus*

Description: 17.5". Plump, small-headed **chickenlike** bird, **black tail with gray tip**. MALE: mostly dark blue-gray with white-spotted sides. FEMALE: complexly patterned brown. **Similar Species:** Ruffed Grouse (above) with black-tipped tail, grayer or more rufous than Sooty, usually in different habitat. White-tailed Ptarmigan (page 87) smaller, white wings and tail. **Status and Habitat**: Conifer forest, dense to open, from lowlands to tree line. **Behavior**: Forages on ground for leaves and buds; conifer needles important in diet. **Voice**: Males make deep, ventriloquial hooting calls from ground or well up in tree. **Did you know?** Sooty Grouse make altitudinal migrations in spring and fall, entirely on foot.

Date & Location Seen: _____

Breeding

Nonbreeding

Description: 12". Small grouse of the high mountains with **white wings and tail. Mottled brown** in summer, male more heavily patterned with black on breast than female; **pure white** in winter.

Similar Species: Much smaller than Sooty Grouse (page 85), which occurs up to treeline. No other chickenlike bird with white wings and tail.

Status and Habitat: Locally common in alpine zone of high Cascades. Trails on Mounts Baker and Rainier (Paradise and Sunrise) best bets, especially in late summer when female has chicks.

Behavior: Individuals and flocks move around among rocks and open areas on foot, feeding on leaves and buds of herbaceous and shrubby plants; add flowers and some insects in summer. Not at all shy but extremely hard to see when not moving, may sit tight as you walk right past them.

Voice: All sorts of chickenlike clucks by both sexes, even one that ends in a sort of scream given in flight.

Did you know? Ptarmigan burrow into the snow to sleep in winter, protected from winds and extreme cold that way.

Date & Location Seen: _____

Description: male 40", wingspan 50"; female 34", wingspan 42". **Very large gallinaceous bird,** dark at a distance but iridescence of most body feathers visible at close range. **Head and neck naked, red to blue**, males with unsightly wattles. Hairlike "beard" on breast, mostly in males.

Similar Species: Nothing else like it. Wild birds usually have buff tail tips, whitish in domestic birds, which originated in Mexico.

Status and Habitat: Long established in San Juan Islands, where common and tame. Also scattered individuals and flocks encountered in wooded parts of lowlands, more common to south and perhaps increasing. Much more common and widespread east of Cascades.

Behavior: Turkeys move around in flocks much of the year and feed on the ground on seeds, including large ones such as acorns. Vary diet with leaves and both invertebrates and small vertebrates such as salamanders. Roost in trees and fly strongly between roosting and feeding areas. Nest on ground in dense vegetation, about a dozen eggs in clutch.

Voice: Everyone knows the classic gobble of the male; great array of other calls, including yelps, cackles, purrs, and staccato alarm calls.

Did you know? This species is one of two worldwide domestic birds that were first domesticated in the New World, Muscovy Duck the other.

Date & Location Seen: _____

Breeding

Nonbreeding

Description: 23", wingspan 30". **Thin bill** appears slightly upcurved, held **tilted slightly upward**. NONBREEDING: **Pale with extensive white on face, throat, and most of neck; gray-brown back speckled with white**. IMMATURE: Entire neck dusky, back markings finer. BREEDING: **Plain brown back,** gray head and neck with fine lines on back, **rufous throat**.

Similar Species: Common Loon (page 95) larger with thicker bill, less white on face and neck in non-breeding plumage. Pacific Loon (page 93) about same size but darker, with straight bill usually held level.

Status and Habitat: Fairly common winter resident on shallow, protected saltwater bays, rarely freshwater lakes. Arrives September, departs by May. More prevalent in northern part of region. Good places to check include Blaine, Fort Flagler State Park, Penn Cove, and west shoreline of Whidbey Island from Point Partridge (Libbey Beach County Park) to Deception Pass.

Behavior: Forages for small fish while diving, often in shallow water. Usually feeds singly or in small flocks, sometimes in large flocks at prey concentrations.

Voice: Silent away from breeding grounds.

Did you know? Red-throated Loon is the only loon that can take flight from land as well as running across the water like other loons.

Date & Location Seen: _____

Breeding

Nonbreeding

Description: 23", wingspan 30". Smooth, **rounded head; slender bill** held horizontally. NONBREEDING: **Dark back**, dark around eye, clean white throat and breast. **Dark back of neck sharply separated from white front; thin, dark chin strap often visible.** IMMATURE: Head paler, back scalloped paler. BREEDING: **Pale gray crown and nape**, black back with white-checkered patches. **Iridescent dark throat and foreneck, white stripes on sides of neck.**

Similar Species: Red-throated Loon (page 91) holds bill slightly upward; more white on neck and face. Common Loon (page 95) larger with thicker bill and steep forehead; in nonbreeding plumage, lacks clean separation between front and back of neck.

Status and Habitat: Fairly common winter resident on open salt water, September–May. Abundant migrant on outer coast. Prefers deeper waters than other loons. More common in northern part of region, for example around Bellingham, Drayton Harbor, San Juan Islands, Point Wilson, and Marrowstone Point; also Cherry Point during April–May herring spawning season.

Behavior: Dives for small fish. Often seen in large, concentrated flocks and feeding with other fish-eaters where strong tidal currents concentrate prey species.

Voice: Calls mainly on breeding grounds.

Did you know? Pacific Loons migrate in flocks, more so than other loons, and thousands move past the outer coast in spring and fall.

Date & Location Seen: _____

Breeding

Nonbreeding

Yellow-billed Loon
Nonbreeding

Description: 30″, wingspan 38″. **Large** loon with **thick bill**, steep forehead. NONBREEDING: White throat and foreneck; back dark brown with lighter mottling. **Dark hindneck looks notched in front**. Bill largely pale. IMMATURE: Back scalloped paler. BREEDING: **Bill, head and neck black with white necklace; dark back checkered white.**

Similar Species: Yellow-billed Loon, *Gavia adamsii*, similar but with yellowish bill (Common's pale with dark ridge on top in nonbreeding plumage) usually held tilted up; head paler than Common's, with dark patch over ear. Red-throated Loon (page 91) more finely built; thin bill held slightly upward. Pacific Loon (page 93) smaller; in non-breeding plumage, sharp contrast between white throat, dark back of neck.

Status and Habitat: Common winter resident anywhere on open salt water or large lakes (a few nonbreeders also in summer). Common on Hood Canal, Drayton Harbor, and Grays Harbor. A few nest on isolated lakes and reservoirs in the lowlands. **Yellow-billed** rare winter visitor anywhere on salt water.

Behavior: Small fish primary prey, also crabs, even occasionally clams. Usually forages singly.

Voice: Distinctive loud yodeling, mostly during breeding season but also sometimes in flight during migration.

Did you know? Nesting Common Loons require pristine conditions and are sensitive to human disturbance.

Date & Location Seen: _____

Breeding

Nonbreeding

Description: 12″. **Brownish, short-necked** grebe with **thick, short, pale bill** and white undertail. BREEDING: Forehead and throat black, **bill with black ring**. Chicks show heavily striped head, red on bill.

Similar Species: Horned and Eared Grebes (pages 99–101) have thinner dark bills, contrasting head and neck in nonbreeding plumage. Red-necked Grebe (page 103) larger with long, mostly yellow bill. American Coot (page 149) adult and juvenile gray rather than brown.

Status and Habitat: Fairly common breeder, becomes common in winter as migrants arrive. Throughout lowlands in marshes, lakes, and ponds, with smaller numbers on protected salt water in winter; also on higher-elevation lakes in migration. Nests in city parks with emergent vegetation, for example Green Lake and Union Bay Marsh (Seattle) and Juanita Bay (Kirkland). Good close looks from auto tour road at Ridgefield National Wildlife Refuge.

Behavior: Dives for small fish, aquatic insects, and crustaceans. To submerge, may dive headfirst or simply allow itself to sink; often resurfaces some distance away, perhaps only with head showing. Not usually in flocks.

Voice: In breeding season, loud *cuck cuck cuck, cow cow cow, cowah cowah cowah.*

Did you know? Pied-billed and other grebes swallow their own feathers, presumably to keep fish bones from penetrating their digestive tract.

Date & Location Seen: _____

Breeding

Nonbreeding

Description: 13.5″. Relatively flat head, red eye, and slender bill with light tip. NONBREEDING: Back, back of neck, and crown brownish black; **front of neck, throat, and cheeks whitish.** BREEDING: Back gray-brown, **neck and sides rufous, head black with golden "horns"** from eye to back of head.

Similar Species: Eared Grebe (page 101) slighter, bill thinner; rides higher in water. In nonbreeding plumage, cheeks dark, top of head peaks above eye. Neck blackish in breeding plumage. Pied-billed Grebe (page 97) overall brownish with thick pale bill. Western Grebe (page 105) larger with longer neck and long, thin bill.

Status and Habitat: Common winter resident (late August–April) on saltwater bays, inlets, and channels; smaller numbers on large freshwater lakes and slow-moving rivers in lowlands.

Behavior: Rides low in water. In winter, feeds mostly on small bottom fish such as gunnels and sculpins obtained by diving. Often in loose flocks. Sometimes attends scoters, which presumably dislodge grebe prey while they forage for mussels. Seen in flight more often than other grebes, white wing patches obvious.

Voice: Mostly silent in winter; high, thin notes occasionally heard.

Did you know? Horned Grebes can stay submerged up to three minutes and swim 500 feet below the surface on one dive.

Date & Location Seen: _____

Breeding

Nonbreeding

Description: 12.5". Petite grebe with **pointed crown**, red eye, floats high in the water. NONBREEDING: **Dusky neck and face**, white throat and patch behind ear. BREEDING: Black neck, puffy crest, and **golden "ears."**

Similar Species: Nonbreeding Horned Grebe (page 99) most similar, has white cheeks and neck, flat head. Nonbreeding Red-necked Grebe (page 103) much larger with long yellow bill. Pied-billed Grebe (page 97) all brown with stubby pale bill.

Status and Habitat: Uncommon migrant and winter visitor throughout lowlands, mostly on protected saltwater bays, smaller numbers on lakes. Often associated with much more common Horned Grebe.

Behavior: Dives to bottom for small fish and invertebrates, more of latter than most grebes. Flies only rarely where resident, almost entirely at night in migration.

Voice: Silent on wintering grounds.

Did you know? Tens of thousands of Eared Grebes gather at Mono Lake and Great Salt Lake to stage for migration. They reduce their flight muscles and become flightless while increasing digestive organ capacity for three months or more. At the end of an intense feeding period, they reduce the size of digestive organs and increase heart and flight muscle to migrate, then reverse this process again after they arrive on their wintering grounds.

Date & Location Seen: _____

Breeding

Nonbreeding

Description: 18″. Large brown grebe with dark eye, **thick neck, tapered yellowish bill.** NONBREEDING: Back and crown dark; **cheek and neck lighter brown, throat white.** BREEDING: **Black crown, reddish neck, pale gray cheeks and throat.** Two white patches on each wing in flight.

Similar Species: More than twice as heavy as Horned (page 99), Eared (page 101), and Pied-billed Grebe (page 97). Horned and Eared have shorter neck, thinner bill, and red eye. Pied-billed brown overall with stubby pale bill. Western Grebe (page 105) same size but with longer, thinner bill and long black and white neck. Red-necked most likely grebe to be mistaken for loon, but neck relatively longer compared with body length.

Status and Habitat: Common winter resident (August–April) on all open marine waters, bays and inlets; few on large lowland lakes. Either side of Admiralty Inlet, Deception Pass State Park, and all over Puget Sound. Lake Washington good freshwater site.

Behavior: Dives for small bottom fish such as gunnels and sculpins. In areas of strong tidal current, flies upcurrent and rides down, then repeats.

Voice: Silent in winter.

Did you know? Red-necked Grebes nest on lakes in northeastern Washington. Like other grebes, they build floating nests and carry their young on their backs.

Date & Location Seen: _____

Western Grebe

Clark's Grebe

Description: 20". **Long-necked, black-and-white** grebe with **long, thin dull yellow bill**. White throat, cheeks, and foreneck; black hindneck. Black cap extends down to include red eye.

Similar Species: Clark's Grebe, *Aechmophorus clarkii*, almost identical but lighter-appearing; bill orange-yellow, dark cap does not cover eye. Nonbreeding Red-necked Grebe (page 103) has shorter gray-brown neck, thicker bill, and dark eye. Nonbreeding Horned Grebe (page 99) similar but much smaller with short neck and smaller dark bill.

Status and Habitat: Common winter resident (September–May) on all saltwater habitats and large lakes. Good numbers usually at Quartermaster Harbor (Vashon–Maury Islands), Drayton Harbor, Hood Canal, Penn Cove, Saratoga Passage (Whidbey–Camano Islands), Elliott Bay in Lake Washington. **Clark's** appear rarely in flocks of Westerns.

Behavior: Mostly schooling fish such as herring and sand lance, obtained by diving. Often forms large flocks in winter. Some birds go through elaborate mating ritual in spring before they migrate to the interior, where they build floating nests on lakes. Almost never seen in flight; migrates at night.

Voice: Loud, high, two-note *crick creeek* call, given all year. **Clark's** call is similar but only single note.

Did you know? Western Grebes are known to follow fish underwater at night by their sparkling trails when bioluminescent algae are present.

Date & Location Seen: _____

Black-footed Albatross

Northern Fulmar

Description: 30", wingspan 74". Large brown gooselike bird with large hooked bill, **very long wings**. **Similar Species**: Much larger than other long-winged seabirds. Laysan Albatross, occasional in same area, is black and white. **Status and Habitat**: Common offshore over open ocean out of sight of land; found throughout summer (April–October). **Behavior**: Glides effortlessly over ocean, beating wings only to take off. Ducks head under to feed on fish and squids at surface, even at night. Solitary except where food aggregated. **Voice**: Generally silent. **Did you know?** Albatrosses breeding in the Hawaiian Islands fly thousands of miles to forage for their single young.

NORTHERN FULMAR *Fulmarus glacialis*

Description: 16", wingspan 36". **Long-winged**, bull-headed seabird, **varies from almost white to medium gray**; stubby yellow bill with **tubular nostrils. Similar Species**: Sooty Shearwater (page 109) darker with longer dark bill not as angled downward. Gulls (pages 209–225) fly differently. **Status and Habitat**: Common offshore visitor, rarely penetrating to Puget Sound; present all year but more common in winter. **Behavior**: Flies with stiff wingbeats alternated with long glides. Assembles in squabbly flocks at good feeding areas. **Voice**: Mostly silent, may give braying or cackling notes in groups. **Did you know?** Northern Fulmars are the only northern-hemisphere nesting species of the petrel family, breeding on cliff ledges in the North Pacific along with kittiwakes and murres.

Date & Location Seen: _____

_____

Description: 17", wingspan 38". **Dark brown long-winged** seabird with **silvery wing linings**, tubular nostrils.

Similar Species: Northern Fulmar (page 107) either white or medium gray, has stubbier bill held pointing downward; wingbeats choppier. Short-tailed Shearwater (rare late fall offshore) slightly smaller with shorter bill and duskier wing linings. Also several other common shearwaters offshore.

Status and Habitat: Abundant during summer (May–October) on outer coast and well offshore, often near enough to shore to be easily observed and penetrating into Willapa Bay and Grays Harbor. Much less common to east in Strait of Juan de Fuca, rarely into Puget Sound, usually later in fall.

Behavior: Huge flocks settling on ocean or flying north or south along coast. Flight rapid, series of rapid wingbeats followed by glide, often ascending well above ocean surface in parabolas during glides. Feeds by shallow dives for surface fish and squids. Attracted to offshore fishing boats discarding bycatch.

Voice: Silent away from breeding grounds.

Did you know? Our Sooty Shearwaters nest in New Zealand and make a long flight into the North Pacific during our summer for their "winter." Some fly east to off South America, then up the Pacific Coast and across to near Japan before making their way back to the burrows on their breeding islands.

Date & Location Seen: _____

_____

Breeding Adult

Immature

Description: 27.5", wingspan 40". **All dark with buffy chin behind dark naked throat skin.** In flight holds neck nearly straight, shows **short tail.** BREEDING: **Blue throat pouch** (visible at close range), fine white plumes on neck and back. IMMATURE: Dark brown with tan breast and belly.

Similar Species: Pelagic Cormorant (page 115) has thinner neck, head, and bill, and longer tail; white flank patch during breeding season. Double-crested Cormorant (page 113) has orange at bill base and throat, longer tail; flies with noticeable crook in neck.

Status and Habitat: Fairly common fall, winter and spring (August–May) on outer coast and in northern part of region, less common in southern Puget Sound. Scarce or absent in nesting season except where it breeds at Cape Disappointment. Common from San Juan Islands ferry, Point Wilson, and Marrowstone Point, among many other sites in protected waters.

Behavior: Dives in open water, primarily feeding on midwater schooling fish. Roosts on rocks and pilings, sometimes in large groups and with other cormorants. On outer coast, flocks fly north in fall to reach our waters, then south in spring, in long lines low over water.

Voice: Usually silent except at nest.

Did you know? Many cormorants have emerald-green eyes, but those of Brandt's are bright blue.

Date & Location Seen: _____

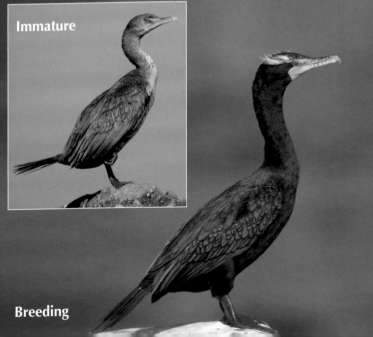

Immature

Breeding

Description: 28", wingspan 42". **All dark** with long neck and tail, pale bill, **orange facial skin and throat pouch.** In flight, **thick neck with pronounced crook**. Emerald green eyes. BREEDING: Paired tufted crests with some white feathers. IMMATURE: Brown with paler (even to whitish) breast and neck.

Similar Species: Brandt's (page 111) and Pelagic (page 115) Cormorants fly with neck held straighter, rarely high in air. Pelagic's bill, head, and neck much thinner. Pelagic has white flank patch in breeding plumage. Brandt's has buffy chin in all plumages.

Status and Habitat: Common resident and local breeder everywhere on coast, both exposed shorelines and bays and estuaries. Also on lakes and rivers, only freshwater cormorant. Large breeding colonies on Protection Island, small islands in San Juans, and islands in Columbia River.

Behavior: Perches on pilings, logs, docks, sandbars, and rocks. Dives for bottom fish. Sometimes flies high in V formation like geese. Swims low in water with head tilted slightly upward. Only cormorant that commonly perches with wings outstretched to dry them.

Voice: Quiet away from breeding grounds.

Did you know? Double-crested Cormorants have increased dramatically in recent decades, and because many of their prey species are important for sport and commerce, they are considered prime "villains" by fishing interests, who have initiated massive control programs.

Date & Location Seen: _____

Breeding

Immature

Description: 25", wingspan 36". **Smallest regional cormorant.** Dark with green and purple sheen (visible in good light). **Slender neck and head, pencil-thin black bill** (like flying snake), green eyes. BREEDING: **White flank patch, red facial skin.** IMMATURE: Uniformly dark brown with brown eyes.

Similar Species: Brandt's Cormorant (page 111) has shorter tail, band of buffy feathers at base of bill. Double-crested Cormorant (page 113) has orange facial skin, flies with crook in thick neck. Pelagic Cormorant slimmer overall than either, with much thinner neck, head, and bill.

Status and Habitat: Locally common breeder and year-round resident along rocky coasts, especially north. Regular on waterfront in major cities. Sizeable nesting colonies on Protection and Minor Islands, few nest on pilings at Anacortes ferry landing. Hard to miss at Point Wilson, Deception Pass State Park, and Westport.

Behavior: Roosts on piers, pilings, bluffs, and rocky shorelines. Dives deep for fish, crustaceans, and other invertebrates. Thought to be capable of diving to over 300 feet. Nests on ledges on cliffsides on islands and mainland.

Voice: Grunts, croaks, and groans on breeding grounds.

Did you know? This and other cormorants acquire their breeding plumes in late winter, hold them through their courtship displays, and lose them soon after they begin nesting.

Date & Location Seen: _____

_____

American White Pelican

Adult

Brown Pelican
Immature

AMERICAN WHITE PELICAN
Pelecanus erythrorhynchos

Description: 55", wingspan 94". **Huge white bird** with big yellow bill and **black flight feathers**. Grows vertical plate on top of bill in breeding season. Head feathers dusky postbreeding. **Similar Species:** None. **Status and Habitat:** Uncommon visitor to region, mostly in summer, on lakes, rivers, and coastal bays. Has nested on Lower Columbia River island. **Behavior:** Captures small fish in pouch while swimming and repeatedly submerging bill. Groups move abreast on water and drive fish in front of them. Flocks often soar high in sky. **Voice:** Silent. **Did you know?** Decimated by DDT, the species has made a great comeback after that pesticide was banned in 1972.

BROWN PELICAN *Pelecanus occidentalis*

Description: 48", wingspan 75". **Large brown bird with big bill and pouch.** ADULT: Gray-brown above, brown below, with white head; hindneck rich dark brown in breeding birds. JUVENILE: Brown above, white below. Three years to maturity, gradual plumage change. **Similar Species:** None. **Status and Habitat:** Abundant in summer on outer coast and in bays and estuaries (May–October), most departed by late fall. **Behavior:** Fly in lines just above the water, birds ascending to dive spectacularly after small schooling fish. Roosts in large numbers on jetties, pilings, and sand islands. **Voice:** Silent. **Did you know?** Seabirds in general are very long-lived, this species at least to 43 years.

Date & Location Seen:

American Bittern

Green Heron

Green Heron

Description: 26", wingspan 39". Stocky **wading bird**, mottled brown above, **brown-striped below**, chartreuse legs. Dark flight feathers contrast with rest of wing. **Similar Species**: Immature Black-crowned Night-Heron (page 125) similar to bittern but with shorter neck and rounder, even-colored wings. **Status and Habitat:** Uncommon resident in freshwater marshes with tall, dense vegetation throughout lowlands. Nisqually and Ridgefield National Wildlife Refuges good locations. **Behavior**: Secretive. Forages mostly at water for fish, frogs, and salamanders. Hides with neck extended, bill pointing up; nests on ground in marsh. **Voice**: Deep pump-like *oong-kah-choonk* in breeding season; squawks in alarm. **Did you know?** A bittern can pluck a flying dragonfly out of the air.

Description: 16", wingspan 24". **Small**, dark **greenish gray,** neck purplish rufous striped with white below, **legs yellow-orange.** IMMATURE: more heavily streaked below. **Similar Species**: Most like crow (page 307) in flight, but note long, pointed front end and cupped wings. **Status and Habitat:** Uncommon summer resident (April–October) in sheltered freshwater ponds, streams and marshes with associated trees; rarely winters. **Behavior**: Forages at water but often from perch rather than wading. Diet small fish and invertebrates. Nests in trees and shrubs. **Voice**: Loud *kyow*. **Did you know?** Green Herons drop plants or other material into the water in front of them to attract small fish.

Date & Location Seen: _____

_____

Description: 40", wingspan 65". **Long-necked, long-legged** wader with formidable **dagger-like bill.** Mostly bluish gray with black and chestnut markings, **white face with long black plumes.** In flight neck pulled in, legs trail behind; wings broad, slightly cupped. IMMATURE: Duller, with dark cap.

Similar Species: Great Egret (page 123) slightly smaller, all white. Black-crowned Night-Heron (page 125) gray, black and white, considerably smaller with short neck and bill. Sandhill Crane (page 151) plainer gray, with "bustle" on back. Typically in pairs or flocks, feeds on land with head down, flies with neck outstretched and loud, bugle-like calls.

Status and Habitat: Common resident throughout at ditches, marshes, ponds, rivers, lakes, estuaries, and open saltwater shore; even croplands and grassy fields.

Behavior: Forages by standing or walking slowly, equally likely in water or fields. Extremely varied diet primarily fish but includes any animal life that can be grasped or speared with bill; voles important component in uplands. Nests primarily in colonies in tall trees.

Voice: Loud croaking, often drawn-out *frahhhnnk*, usually given when flushed or chasing another heron.

Did you know? Great Blue Herons often desert nesting colonies when harassed by Bald Eagles, which have increased greatly in the region and pose a significant threat to heron populations.

Date & Location Seen: _____

Description: 36", wingspan 50". Large **pure white heron** with long bright **yellow bill**, long neck, and long **black legs**. Bill develops black on upper mandible and green on lores during breeding.

Similar Species: Nothing else like it. Snowy Egret, immature Little Blue Heron, and Cattle Egret all white herons but much smaller and very rare. Great Blue Heron (page 121) can look pale at a distance.

Status and Habitat: Uncommon to fairly common resident in southwestern part of region in Vancouver area and north along coast to Grays Harbor. Disperses northward from there at any time of year, most common in region late summer and fall. Probability of sighting declines northward, rare in northern part of region. A few pairs have bred at Ridgefield National Wildlife Refuge.

Behavior: Wades in shallow water for fish and stalks voles in grassland, much like Great Blue Heron.

Voice: Fairly loud *frahnk*, like subdued Great Blue Heron call, when disturbed.

Did you know? A century ago egrets were hunted for their plumes, the fancy feathers they grow when breeding. Their decline in numbers were in part responsible for major conservation programs, including the origin of the National Audubon Society and the Migratory Bird Treaty Act.

Date & Location Seen: _____

_____

Immature

Description: 24", wingspan 39". Mostly gray and white small heron with **black crown and back**. White head plume and large, bright red eye. IMMATURE: **Brown**, heavily streaked with white. Gradual plumage change, two-year old plain gray with darker crown.

Similar Species: No other bird is similarly black and gray above. American Bittern (page 119) brown like immature but lacking white spots on back and wings and with longer, more prominently striped neck. Bittern much shyer and usually in cover, two-toned wings obvious in flight.

Status and Habitat: Rather rare migrant and winter visitor at ponds and marshes, potentially anywhere in lowlands. Have been winter roost sites at Fir Island and Warm Beach. Much more common east of Cascades.

Behavior: Forages at water on fish, frogs, and crayfish. Most feeding done at night but sometimes active during day, when often seen resting at waterside. Unlike bitterns, night-herons roost in trees, sometimes in groups.

Voice: Single hollow *wok*, usually given in flight; startling when out of the night sky.

Did you know? Black-crowned Night-Herons are among the most wide-ranging bird species, occurring on all continents except Antarctica and in addition many oceanic islands.

Date & Location Seen: _____

Description: 24", wingspan 60". **Blackish**, long-tailed, with small, bare **red head**; soars on long, fairly broad, two-toned **wings held above horizontal** in tipping, unsteady flight. IMMATURE: Black head.

Similar Species: Eagles (pages 131, 145) and Red-tailed Hawk (page 141) soar with wings held flatter (Golden Eagle somewhat elevated); heads larger, different underwing patterns. Northern Harrier (page 133) also with wings up in flight but much smaller, flies low, and rump white.

Status and Habitat: Fairly common but local summer resident in forested lowlands, rarely up to mountain passes. Also forages in nearby clearings, only rarely in urban areas. Numbers augmented by migrants, especially in fall. Arrives March, most depart October. Best bets include east side of Olympics, Chehalis River valley, and San Juan Islands.

Behavior: Soars, searching for dead animals by sight and smell. Seldom flaps, relying on thermals for lift. Gregarious, usually roosting, migrating, and feeding in groups. Reluctantly crosses water bodies in migration, waiting for favorable winds, resulting at times in concentrated migratory flights.

Voice: Grunting and hissing (seldom heard).

Did you know? Turkey Vultures have an impressive sense of smell, able to find dead animals as small as mice hidden under the forest canopy. Local birds migrate all the way to Panama and beyond for the winter.

Date & Location Seen: _____

Male

Female

Description: 22", wingspan 60". **Dark brown above** except for mostly **white crown. White underparts** contrast with **dark mask**, strongly barred wings and tail. Wings long, held somewhat angled (gull-like), with dark patch at wrist. MALE: Breast all white. FEMALE: Breast marked with brown. JUVENILE: Speckled with white above.

Similar Species: Immature Bald Eagle (page 131) in transitional plumage never has entirely white underparts but may show dark mask on white head. Hawks have shorter wings, gulls more pointed wings.

Status and Habitat: Fairly common and increasing summer resident, arriving late March and most departing by October. Usually at water, including rivers, lakes and estuaries; migrants may be anywhere overhead. High concentration at Everett waterfront.

Behavior: Feeds almost exclusively on live fish, hovering over water and plunging feet first, sometimes catching prey well below surface. Pairs build bulky nest on top of broken tree, power tower, or platform, often near human habitation. May be loosely colonial.

Voice: Noisy, calling with slurred, shrill whistles *chirp, chirp, chirp.*

Did you know? This unique species, sometimes classified in a family of its own, is highly adapted for fishing, with long wings to lift heavy fish from the water and rough soles to hold onto them.

Date & Location Seen: _____

Adult

Subadult

Immature

Description: 32", wingspan 75". ADULT: Dark brown with **white head and tail**; bill, eye, and huge feet yellow. JUVENILE: Entirely brown, **much white under wings**, bill and eye dark. Changes gradually to adult plumage over four years, underparts partially white during this. Soars on long, broad wings.

Similar Species: Hawks smaller with relatively shorter wings. Golden Eagle (page 145) has golden feathers on nape, white patches farther out on wings, and white-based tail until maturity; flies with wings angled up slightly. Turkey Vulture (page 127) much smaller, small-headed, flies with two-toned wings angled up even more.

Status and Habitat: Fairly common and increasing resident, numbers augmented in winter by migrants. Nests in large trees near water. Concentrates along rivers in early winter (Skagit River near Rockport good), later along coastlines and on lakes. Flies over urban areas.

Behavior: Feeds mostly on fish, including spawned-out salmon. Hunts water birds regularly and feeds on carrion of all sorts. Commonly steals food from other raptors. Pairs return to territories in fall. Eggs laid by early March, young fledge in July.

Voice: Far-carrying series of chirping whistles.

Did you know? After breeding, many Bald Eagles track salmon, moving to more northerly rivers for early spawning runs and then moving southward for winter runs in our region.

Date & Location Seen: _____

Male

Juvenile

Female

Description: 18", wingspan 38". Slim, **long-winged**, with **owl-like face**, long, banded tail, **white rump**. Usually flies with **wings held above horizontal**, rocking from side to side. MALE: Gray (whiter below, dotted with reddish brown) with black wingtips. FEMALE: Larger; brown above, streaked below. IMMATURE: Resembles female but orangish below, lacking streaks.

Similar Species: White rump and flight style distinctive. Rough-legged Hawk (page 143) has white tail base, not rump. Red-tailed Hawk (page 141) has broader wings. Cooper's Hawk (page 137) smaller, holds shorter wings flat. Falcons (pages 275–281) have more pointed wings, swifter flight.

Status and Habitat: Locally common migrant and winter resident in open country, including marshes, fields, and agricultural flats. Uncommon breeder in lowlands, usually associated with marshy wetlands.

Behavior: Courses low, "harries" prey, using both eyes and ears to locate movement, then dives to flush and catch small mammals and birds. May hover briefly. Concentrates at productive locations to hunt and roost. Persistently chases Short-eared Owls to steal prey. Nests on ground.

Voice: Calls include whistles, also rapid chatter heard while breeding, occasionally on winter quarters.

Did you know? Male Northern Harriers may mate with several females. Courting pairs perform spectacular roller-coaster flights and prey transfers high in the air.

Date & Location Seen: _____

Immature

Adult

SHARP-SHINNED HAWK
Accipiter striatus

Description: 12", wingspan 22" (female larger than male). **Small, slim, short-winged hawk with long, thin yellow legs, long, square-tipped tail** with broad bands. Alternates rapid flapping with gliding. ADULT: Head and back gray, barred reddish brown below, eye bright red. IMMATURE: Brownish back, streaked brown on white below. Eye yellow.

Similar Species: Cooper's Hawk (page 137) nearly identical but larger, tail rounder at tip; adult has "capped," more square-headed appearance. Size separation tricky—female Sharp-shinned not much smaller than male Cooper's. American Kestrel (page 275) and Merlin (page 277) have pointed wings.

Status and Habitat: Fairly common migrant throughout, less common in winter. Associated with forest but occurs widely in migration, including urban and suburban settings. Uncommon breeder in dense conifer forest in mountains.

Behavior: Feeds almost exclusively on small birds, often at bird feeders. Bursts forth from hidden perch to surprise prey in low, rapid flight, pivots forward to strike with long legs. Often shadows migrating songbird flocks. Pugnacious if concealed nest discovered.

Voice: Series of high-pitched *kews*.

Did you know? Male and female accipiter hawks are very different in size, allowing a pair to feed on a much greater variety of prey within their nesting territory.

Date & Location Seen: _____

Immature

Adult

Description: 16.5", wingspan 27" female larger than male). Lanky hawk with long, yellow legs and **long, broadly banded rounded tail**. Alternates flapping and gliding; soars with wings extended straight out. ADULT: **Dark gray cap**, grayish back, pale gray neck, barred reddish brown below, reddish eye. IMMATURE: Brown above, white with brown streaks below. Eye yellow.

Similar Species: Sharp-shinned Hawk (page 135) almost identical but smaller, tail roughly square at tip. Adult lacks "capped" appearance, soars with wrists held forward. Male Cooper's only slightly larger than female Sharp-shinned. Red-tailed Hawk (page 141) bulkier with relatively shorter tail, narrow tail bands. Northern Goshawk (page 139) adult gray, immature streaked below, both with white eye-line.

Status and Habitat: Fairly common resident throughout in forest, open woodland, widely in cities; additional migrants come into region in winter. Secretive nester, much more evident in other seasons.

Behavior: Ambushes prey from hidden perch with rapid burst of speed, also searches while cruising; often stakes out bird feeders. Takes mostly birds, also small mammals such as rats when nesting. Disperses widely in fall although many remain year-round in breeding range.

Voice: Calls include repeated *kek*, nasal squawks.

Did you know? Accipiters use thermals to assist in travel during migration and to locate prey while soaring.

Date & Location Seen: _____

Adult

Immature

Description: 22", wingspan 37" (female larger than male). **Large forest hawk** with **white line over eye**, long barred tail. ADULT: gray above, darker around head, gray-barred below. Eye red. IMMATURE: brown above, white heavily streaked with brown below. Eye yellow.

Similar Species: No other regional hawk has prominent white eye-line. Immature Cooper's Hawk (page 137) similar but smaller. Immature Red-tailed Hawk (page 141) similar to immature but with relatively shorter tail, different flight style. Harrier (page 133) with longer wings, white rump patch.

Status and Habitat: Uncommon resident in mountain conifer forest; even less common as migrant and winter visitor to wooded and more open parts of lowlands.

Behavior: Alternates rapid flapping and gliding in flight. Forages in and around forest for hares and grouse, may capture anything in that size range. Usually hunts from a perch, then chases prey through forest, amazingly agile at flying among tree branches. Otherwise often seen soaring overhead. Accipiters are fierce predators, and this is the fiercest.

Voice: Vocal with *ki-ki-ki-ki* or *kak-kak-kak* calls when nesting, silent otherwise.

Did you know? Goshawks migrate out of their northern breeding areas about every 10 years, corresponding to low years in snowshoe hare and grouse populations.

Date & Location Seen: _____

Adult

Immature

Adult

Description: 21", wingspan 46". Bulky. Soars on **broad wings** held flat. **Dark line on leading edge of underwing** from neck to wrist, **dark head,** pale breast, **streaked band across belly.** ADULT: Reddish tail. IMMATURE: Brown above, finely banded tail, whiter breast. DARK MORPH: Adult reddish to brown except lighter flight feathers. HARLAN'S subspecies: Usually blackish, lacking brown tones, or very white below; tail whitish to gray, may show reddish.

Similar Species: Rough-legged Hawk (page 143) has white tail with black tip, whitish head, dark wrist marks on underwings, often hovers. Eagles (pages 131, 145) larger with longer wings.

Status and Habitat: Most common and widespread hawk in region, in open and edge habitats, including freeway corridors and clearcuts. Numbers augmented by migrants and wintering birds. Dark morph uncommon; Harlan's quite uncommon winter visitor.

Behavior: Hunts for wide variety of prey, mostly from perch, dropping to capture prey in talons. Also soars, sometimes "kites" in stationary hover in wind. Will take carrion. Protects territory year-round, calling at intruders.

Voice: Most common call rasping, down-slurred scream.

Did you know? Red-tailed Hawks come in an amazing assortment of plumages. Variation among regional populations, color morphs, ages, and even individuals can make this common species difficult to identify.

Date & Location Seen: _____

_____

Description: 21", wingspan 48". Broad-winged soaring hawk with **variable plumage** dependent on sex, age, and color morph. Key marks include small bill, **whitish head and upper breast** contrasting with **dark belly**; white underwings with **dark wrist patches, white tail with wide black band at tip** (female). MALE: Black tail band narrower, sometimes additional bands. IMMATURE: Tail band ill-defined. Less common dark morph all blackish except for mostly white flight feathers.

Similar Species: Red-tailed Hawk (page 141) immature may appear similar, especially when hovering, but belly streaked instead of solid dark and underwing lacks wrist mark, instead coverts form dark leading edge.

Status and Habitat: Fairly common winter resident (October–April) in agricultural fields, prairies, and beachside dunes in lowlands, migrants also in mountains. Good bets include Samish Flats, Nisqually National Wildlife Refuge.

Behavior: Hunts for small mammals from perch or in flight; also takes birds on arctic breeding grounds. Commonly hunts by hovering with rapidly beating wings. Often perches on branches that appear small for its bulk, very often on utility wires and posts. Also perches on open ground, as do many other hawks.

Voice: Seldom heard except when nesting.

Did you know? As in most other raptors, young birds have considerably lower foraging success than adults.

Date & Location Seen: _____

_____

Adult

Immature

Description: 33", wingspan 75". **Large dark brown bird of prey with long, broad wings**, held up at slight angle in flight. **Golden feathers** on back of head, wing and tail feathers subtly barred. Lower legs feathered. IMMATURE: Big white patches two-thirds way out wing, tail base widely white. White areas diminish with successive molts over four years to maturity.

Similar Species: Bald Eagle (page 131) same size but head looks bigger; adult with white head and tail, immatures mostly brown but much white in underwing coverts and often white on underparts; lower legs bare. Wings held flat rather than elevated. Soaring hawks (pages 141–143) much smaller with shorter wings.

Status and Habitat: Small numbers in higher open country in Olympics and Cascades; small resident population in San Juan Islands, otherwise occasional winter visitor anywhere in lowlands.

Behavior: Soars high in air or low over open hillsides looking for prey, mostly medium-sized mammals such as rabbits and marmots but also birds. Big nest usually on cliff ledge, used year after year. Very territorial, not gregarious like Bald Eagle.

Voice: Yelping and mewing calls in breeding season, not very vocal away from nest.

Did you know? On the steppes of Asia, Golden Eagles are used to hunt foxes from horseback.

Date & Location Seen: _____

Virginia Rail

Sora

Description: 8.5". Shy long-legged marsh bird with **reddish-brown breast**, gray face, **long, thin, slightly downcurved red bill**, barred black and white flanks, and short tail (often cocked upward). **Similar Species**: Sora (below) has short yellow bill, adult with gray breast and black face. **Status and Habitat**: Fairly common summer resident, uncommon winter resident. Usually in cattail marshes. **Behavior**: Eats small animals of all kinds, from insects to frogs; some plant material. Probes with bill in mud and shallow water. Runs or walks, staying well hidden. **Voice**: Calls include *kiddik kiddik kiddik* in breeding season; series of grunts, often in duet, throughout year. **Did you know?** Rails have very narrow breastbone and pelvis to thread their way through dense vegetation.

SORA *Porzana carolina*

Description: 7". Skulking marsh bird with brown-streaked back, gray breast, black and white barred flanks, and **short yellow bill and black face.** IMMATURE: Brownish without black on face. **Similar Species**: Virginia Rail (above) reddish with long reddish bill. **Status and Habitat**: Fairly common summer resident in sedge and grass marshes. **Behavior**: Skulks through vegetation, regularly out in open as water levels drop in late summer. Picks up invertebrates and seeds from mud or water. **Voice**: A loud *prree, preee, preee* followed by descending and slowing whinny. **Did you know?** Long toes aid in walking on marsh vegetation.

Date & Location Seen: _____

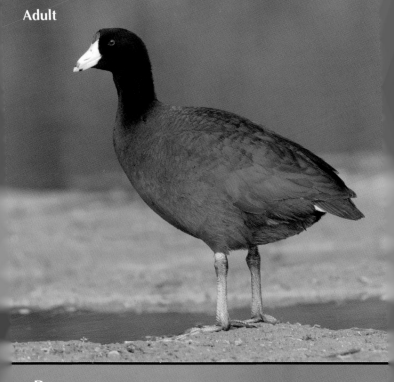

Adult

Downy

Description: 13″. **Dark gray ducklike** bird, undertail edged in white. **Black head, red eyes, pointed white bill** with black marks near tip (dark red shield at base). Legs greenish, **long lobed toes**. JUVENILE: Paler head and neck, dusky bill. Downy young with bill and frizzy down on head and neck red.

Similar Species: : Distinctive bill and swimming style distinguish coots from ducks. Pied-billed Grebe (page 97) brown.

Status and Habitat: Locally fairly common summer resident, common winter resident (September–March) in lowlands. Breeds in shallow freshwater lakes and wetlands with emergent vegetation. Winters on open water of lakes, ponds, and protected saltwater bays. Present in all seasons in Union Bay Marsh (Lake Washington, Seattle).

Behavior: Swims like a chicken might, with pumping head (ducks don't do this). Dives or tips up in shallow water, grazes on lawns and meadows. Eats mostly plants, also a few small aquatic animals. Very gregarious, often forming large rafts. Needs long takeoff run, splashing strides on water until airborne.

Voice: *Puck* notes singly or in series; array of other cackling, clucking, and crowing calls.

Did you know? Coots feed their young, unlike ducks, and the bright heads and bills of the downies allow the adults to keep track of them in aquatic vegetation.

Date & Location Seen: _____

Description: 32", wingspan 64". **Large, long-billed, long-necked and long-legged** prairie bird. **Gray** all over with red semi-feathered crown. Inner wing feathers (tertials) long and floppy, producing "**bustle**" over tail.

Similar Species: Only Great Blue Heron (page 121) similar. Heron often feeds in water, not in flocks, no bustle, slow and steady flight with wings curved down, neck pulled in.

Status and Habitat: Winters locally in open fields and meadows along Lower Columbia River, especially Ridgefield National Wildlife Refuge and Vancouver bottoms. Otherwise uncommon migrant on outer coast, small groups or individuals rare possibility anywhere in lowlands. Healthy breeding population at Conboy Lake National Wildlife Refuge at southeast edge of the Puget Sound Region.

Behavior: Strides over open areas hunting for large invertebrates and small vertebrates, including rodents and nestling birds. Forms large flocks in migration and winter, often high in air. Flies with neck outstretched and upward flip of wingtips. "Dancing" behavior common, individuals and pairs posturing and leaping into the air.

Voice: Loud, bugling calls.

Did you know? Cranes, like geese and swans, mate for life and travel in family groups. Our breeding birds are "Greater" Sandhill Cranes, perceptibly larger than the "Lesser" Sandhill Cranes that come here from their Arctic breeding grounds.

Date & Location Seen: _____

_____

151

Description: 16". **Chunky, dark brown and black** shorebird with long, chisel-like **bright red bill**, red eye-ring, golden eye. Relatively short pinkish legs. Female has spot on iris lacking in male. IMMATURE: Brown-tipped bill.

Similar Species: Nothing else like this showy species. May roost with bill tucked under wing, less easily identified then.

Status and Habitat: Uncommon resident. Limited to rocky coastline on outer coast and in northern part of region. Good spots include Salt Creek Recreation Area, Semiahmoo Spit, San Juan Islands, and Deception Pass State Park. Rarely south in Puget Sound and south of Point Grenville on outer coast. Prefers rocky shores, islets, cobble beaches, jetties, and breakwaters.

Behavior: Forages mostly when tide low, primarily for limpets, mussels, and other shellfish. Uses laterally compressed bill to pry shells apart or off rocks. Usually in pairs or family groups but can come together in large roosts outside breeding season. Nonmigratory but disperses infrequently to coastal localities away from nesting grounds.

Voice: Loud, ringing *wheeep wheeep*; rolling series given in spectacular courtship display.

Did you know? It must be difficult to be an oystercatcher until the bill is fully grown, as the young are fed by their parents until they fledge, unusual for a shorebird.

Date & Location Seen: _____

Breeding Male

Nonbreeding

Description: 11". Plump-looking, with **short bill**, relatively short blackish legs. BREEDING: Adults show **black face, breast, and belly,** whitish crown, neck, sides, and undertail, spangled back. Female browner, less distinctly marked. NONBREEDING: Light brown above with darker markings, indistinct whitish eyebrow, brownish breast and white belly; **black axillars** (armpits) visible in flight. JUVENILE: Browner, with white-spangled upperparts

Similar Species: Distinctive in breeding plumage, bill shorter than other large shorebirds. American and Pacific Golden-Plovers (page 157) slightly smaller, more golden in summer; browner, lack black axillars in fall.

Status and Habitat: Fairly common migrant and winter resident (July–May), almost entirely at salt water. Most common on outer coast, as at Grays Harbor and Willapa Bay, fewer in protected waters. Locally common at Dungeness and on Skagit Bay. Feeds on beaches and mudflats, moves onto short-grass and plowed fields at high tides.

Behavior: Forages visually by running, stopping, and picking food from substrate. Diet mostly worms and other marine invertebrates, also insects in fields. Birds spread out to feed but roost in groups, often flocking with other shorebirds, especially Dunlins.

Voice: Very vocal. Most common call forlorn-sounding, whistled *pleeoweee*.

Did you know? This widespread species is known in Eurasia as the Grey Plover.

Date & Location Seen: _____

American Golden-Plover
Breeding Male

American Golden-Plover
Juvenile

Pacific Golden-Plover
Breeding Male

Pacific Golden-Plover
Nonbreeding

Description: 10". Medium-sized shorebirds with **short bills, gold-spangled upperparts**. BREEDING: Males of both with **black breasts and bellies; American** black throughout, **Pacific** with white on sides and undertail. Females duller. NON-BREEDING: Both very similar, **Pacific** remains gold-spotted, **American** becomes plain. JUVENILE: Extremely similar, **American** wings extending farther beyond tail tip and **Pacific** longer-legged, toes extending beyond tail in flight.

Similar Species: Black-bellied Plover (page 155) larger with larger bill; marked with white above and more white under tail in breeding, also white wing stripe and black axillars in flight.

Status and Habitat: Both species uncommon migrants (May and August–October), mostly on outer coast beaches, bays, and estuaries. **Pacific** most likely species in spring and early fall, both more common later in fall when represented by juveniles. **Pacific** lingers a bit longer and very rarely winters.

Behavior: Run, stop and pick from surface in typical plover fashion. Both feed up in vegetation of salt marshes more often than Black-bellied. Among fastest-flying of birds.

Voice: Both call in flight, *chu-weedle* by **American** and a shorter *chu-wi* by **Pacific**.

Did you know? Both species breed side by side in western Alaska; after breeding, Americans head for Patagonia and Pacifics for the South Pacific.

Date & Location Seen: _____

Snowy Plover
Breeding

Semipalmated Plover
Breeding

Description: 7". **Light gray-brown** plover with **short black bill,** short **tan legs.** BREEDING: Black line across forehead, black smudge on side of breast. **Similar Species:** Semipalmated Plover (below) darker, with breast band and yellow-orange legs. **Status and Habitat:** Local and uncommon resident on sand beaches on outer coast from Midway Beach south. Leadbetter Point best. **Behavior:** Runs and stops to pick invertebrates from surface. Often runs rather than flies to escape disturbance. **Voice:** Fairly quiet when flushed, often gives churred calls when breeding. **Did you know?** Snowy Plovers are considered Endangered in Washington, and some beaches are closed while they are nesting.

SEMIPALMATED PLOVER *Charadrius semipalmatus*

Description: 7". Plain brown above except for **white collar,** black forehead and cheek; white below with **black breast band**. Short bill with **orange base**; short **yellow-orange legs**. White wing stripe visible in flight. JUVENILE: Duller, with dark bill. **Similar Species:** Darker than Snowy Plover (above). Large downy Killdeer (page 161) may have single band, usually looks gawky. **Status and Habitat:** Fairly common coastal migrant (April–May, July–October), a few winter. Best spots Grays Harbor, Willapa Bay. Common on beaches and mudflats. **Behavior:** Forages visually by running, stopping, and picking food from substrate. Feeds on marine invertebrates, especially worms. **Voice:** Common flight call sharp whistled *chuwee*. **Did you know?** Semipalmated Plover gets its name from its partially webbed feet.

Date & Location Seen: _____

Description: 10". Plain brown above with white collar and underparts, **two black breast bands**. Forehead and eyebrow white, eye-ring scarlet, **bill short and dark**; legs relatively short, tan. **Orange rump** and tail base and white wing stripe visible in flight. Downy young with one breast band when half-grown.

Similar Species: Semipalmated Plover (page 159) smaller with single breast band, shorter bill, lacks orange rump.

Status and Habitat: Common summer resident, less common in winter. Mostly lowlands, also up major river valleys to moderate elevations. Open habitats without high grass: lawns, road edges, beaches, plowed fields, and parking lots; mudflats in winter. Prefers bare gravel near water for nesting.

Behavior: Forages visually by running, stopping, and picking food from ground. Often active at night. Feeds mostly on insects, also marine invertebrates at coast. Secretive at exposed nest site but calls and feigns broken wing as part of distraction display when discovered. Flocks concentrate in farm fields in late summer.

Voice: Varied strident calls include *deee, deee*, and high, rapid trill when nervous. Loud *killdeer, killdeer* calls by male in "butterfly" display flight when breeding.

Did you know? The Killdeer's four black-blotched tan or greenish eggs are nearly invisible in their gravel nest when left unattended.

Date & Location Seen: _____

Spotted Sandpiper
Breeding

Spotted Sandpiper
Juvenile

Solitary Sandpiper
Breeding

Solitary Sandpiper
Juvenile

Description: 7″. Small, brown, **short yellow bill**, short tan legs, **short white wing stripe, constant teetering motion**. BREEDING: **Black spots** on white underparts. NONBREEDING: No spots, **white extends in front of folded wing**. JUVENILE: Buff bars on wing coverts. **Similar Species**: Solitary Sandpiper (below) darker, with fine white or buff spotting, no white eye-line. **Status and Habitat:** Fairly common summer resident (April–September), uncommon in winter. Nests on all freshwater shores, up into mountains. Locally at salt water after breeding. **Behavior**: Forages by picking invertebrates from substrate. Highly territorial throughout year. Flies with wings fluttering below horizontal, alternating with glides. **Voice**: Loud, clear, high-pitched whistles. **Did you know?** Spotted Sandpiper females often mate with more than one male.

SOLITARY SANDPIPER *Tringa solitaria*

Description: Description: 8″. Very **dark, short-billed** sandpiper with greenish legs. **Dark wings** and **white-edged tail** in flight. **Similar Species**: Spotted Sandpiper (above) teeters, lighter brown. Yellowlegs (page 167) larger with longer yellow legs, pale underwings, and whitish tail. **Status and Habitat**: Uncommon spring (April–May) and fall (July–September) migrant throughout in freshwater ponds and marshes. **Behavior**: Always solitary, feeding in same habitat as yellowlegs. When flushed, usually flies high in air and disappears. **Voice**: High-pitched repeated whistles. **Did you know?** Solitary Sandpiper is our only shorebird that nests in old songbird nests in trees.

Date & Location Seen: _____

Wandering Tattler
Breeding

Wandering Tattler
Juvenile

Rock Sandpiper
Breeding

Rock Sandpiper
Nonbreeding

Description: 11". Straight-billed **gray** sandpiper with **short yellow legs, plain wings and tail**. BREEDING: Heavily barred below. JUVENILE: No bars below, faint filigree pattern on upper-parts. **Similar Species**: No other sandpiper gunmetal gray. Other rock shorebirds much more patterned. **Status and Habitat**: Common spring (April–May) and fall (July–September) migrant on rocky shores of outer coasts. Much smaller numbers in protected waters. **Behavior**: Feeds on rock substrate by picking invertebrates out of crevices and masses of seaweeds. Solitary. **Voice**: Series of loud, ringing notes when disturbed. **Did you know?** Wandering Tattlers are ocean goers, spreading all over the tropical Pacific in the nonbreeding season.

ROCK SANDPIPER *Calidris ptilocnemis*

Description: 7". NONBREEDING: Small sandpiper with gray back and breast, **heavily spotted sides**, short, yellow-based bill and **short yellow legs**. BREEDING: Reddish brown back, dark ear patch, **black breast patch**; bill and legs dark. **Similar Species**: Dunlin (page 181) similar but bill longer, brown in winter, light rufous back and black belly patch in spring. Other rock shorebirds with different bills. **Status and Habitat**: Uncommon winter resident (October–May) on rocky outer coast, much less common in protected waters. **Behavior**: Picks invertebrates from algal mats and rock surface. Often flocks with Black Turnstones and Surfbirds. **Voice**: Quiet in migration. **Did you know?** Rock Sandpipers winter farther north than any other of our shorebirds.

Date & Location Seen:

**Greater Yellowlegs
Breeding**

**Greater Yellowlegs
Juvenile**

**Lesser Yellowlegs
Breeding**

**Lesser Yellowlegs
Juvenile**

Description: 12" / 10.5 ". Elegant grayish waders with **long, bright yellow legs**, long neck, fairly long and mostly dark bill, patterned upperparts and breast. White below, with **plain wings and whitish tail** visible in flight. BREEDING: Breast and back marked with black. JUVENILE: Darker above with pale markings. **Greater** more robust, with **longer, slightly upturned bill**, pale-based in winter. **Lesser** more delicate; **bill shorter, straighter, always black**.

Similar Species: Solitary Sandpiper (page 163) smaller and darker, with shorter, greenish legs. Willet (page 169) larger, with gray legs.

Status and Habitat: Fairly common migrants. **Greater** March–May and July–September; a few remain for winter. **Lesser** July–October, much less common in spring (May). Both occur in flooded fields, marshes, ponds, estuaries, and tidal flats. **Lesser** less likely in saltwater habitat.

Behavior: Both forage in shallow water, swinging bill side to side or running after small fish, insects, and other invertebrates. Roost in loose groups.

Voice: Call *tew*, repeated 3–4 times in **Greater**, usually 2 times, less musical and lower pitched, in **Lesser**; both *tew* continuously in alarm.

Did you know? Greater Yellowlegs nests in the muskeg wetlands all across the Alaskan and Canadian boreal forest. The nest is almost impossible to find, so breeding biology is poorly known.

Date & Location Seen: _____

Willet

Willet
Breeding

Willet
Nonbreeding

Whimbrel
Adult

Description: 13.5". **Large sandpiper with straight bill**, blue-gray legs, **black and white wing pattern**. BREEDING: Heavily barred with black and brown. NONBREEDING: Plain gray-brown. JUVENILE: Mottled buff and brown above. **Similar Species**: Other large shorebirds have longer upturned or decurved bills. None of them with vivid flight pattern. **Status and Habitat**: Small flock winters (September–April) at Tokeland, Willapa Bay. Rare elsewhere. **Behavior**: Picks and probes from surface of mud or water. High-tide roosts on pilings. **Voice**: Rather silent in winter, occasionally a musical *kay-whuh*. **Did you know?** Like many other sandpipers, Willets "sing" in display flight on their breeding grounds.

WHIMBREL *Numenius phaeopus*

Description: 16". **Large and brown**, with **long decurved bill, dark brown head stripes**. Back mottled; belly paler, unmarked. JUVENILE: pale spots on darker back. **Similar Species:** Long-billed Curlew (page 171) larger, longer-billed, with cinnamon underwings. Marbled Godwit (page 171) with long, upturned bill. **Status and Habitat:** Fairly common spring (May), uncommon fall (July–September) migrant on salt water. Mudflats, rocky shores, and salt marshes. **Behavior**: Forages by picking or probing for crabs and worms. Large spring flocks drawn to newly plowed wet fields; fall migrants alone or in smaller groups. **Voice**: Loud *whi whi whi whi whi* whistle, also trills in spring. **Did you know?** The curved bill is perfect for extracting crabs from burrows.

Date & Location Seen: _____

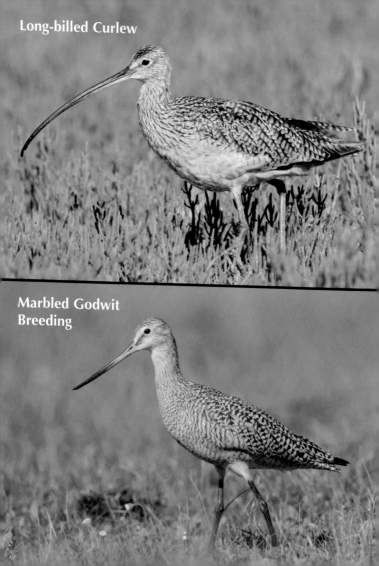

Long-billed Curlew

Marbled Godwit
Breeding

LONG-BILLED CURLEW
Numenius americanus

Description: 21". **Very large reddish brown** sandpiper with **long decurved bill** (longer in female). Heavily marked with dark brown above, wings reddish in flight. **Similar Species**: Marbled Godwit (below) smaller with straight bill. Whimbrel (page 169) smaller with dark head stripes, no hint of reddish. **Status and Habitat**: Rather rare spring (April) and fall (July–August) migrant on salt water; small flock winters near Tokeland. **Behavior**: Advances rapidly over mudflats, looking for crabs and other burrowing invertebrates that it can extract with its bill. **Voice**: Loud *curlee* occasionally given. **Did you know?** Most Long-billed Curlews winter on salt water, but many do so in interior grasslands, habitats like their breeding grounds.

MARBLED GODWIT *Limosa fedoa*

Description: 17". **Large reddish brown sandpiper** with **long, slightly upturned bill**. BREEDING: Dark bars on underparts. NONBREEDING, JUVENILE: Plain underparts. **Similar Species**: No other common large sandpipers have a bill like this. **Status and Habitat**: Winter resident (August–May) on bays and estuaries in Willapa Bay and Grays Harbor, where much increased in recent years. Rare migrant elsewhere on salt water. **Behavior**: Feeds on mudflats by probing deeply with head down. Roosts and feeds in much larger groups than curlews. **Voice**: Abrupt calls *ta-wit ta-wit* ("godwit"). **Did you know?** Most Marbled Godwits nest on the Great Plains, but ours come from a population breeding in southern Alaska.

Date & Location Seen: _____

Ruddy Turnstone
Breeding Male

Ruddy Turnstone
Nonbreeding

Black Turnstone
Breeding

Black Turnstone
Nonbreeding

RUDDY TURNSTONE
Arenaria interpres

Description: 9″. Short **chisel-like bill, black breast pattern, orange legs**, showy flight pattern. BREEDING: Bright **rufous and black above**, females duller. NONBREEDING: Mottled brown above. **Similar Species:** Black Turnstone (below) black and white. No other shorebirds have such short, pointed bills. **Status and Habitat:** Fairly common spring (May) and uncommon fall (July–September) migrant on outer coast shores and bays, less common on protected waters. Uses all substrates, mud to sand to rocks. **Behavior:** Very active. Flips over stones and seaweed to find animals beneath. Often forages in oyster beds. **Voice:** Musical chatter while foraging or in flight. **Did you know?** This worldwide migrant sometimes feeds on seabird eggs and carrion.

BLACK TURNSTONE *Arenaria melanocephala*

Description: 9″. Short **chisel-like bill,** brownish legs, **black and white** flight pattern. BREEDING: Mostly black, white patches above and below eye. NONBREEDING: Browner, without face markings. **Similar Species:** Larger Surfbird (page 177) lacks white back patches in flight. Ruddy Turnstone (above) has orange legs, harlequin pattern in breeding plumage, brown in winter. **Status and Habitat:** Fairly common migrant and winter resident on rocky shores (mid July–April). **Behavior:** Forages on rocks, prying off mussels and other marine invertebrates. **Voice:** Noisy, with shrill rattles, especially when flushed. **Did you know?** Black Turnstones act as sentinels, calling frequently in alarm, and Surfbirds with them respond by flying.

Date & Location Seen: _____

Breeding

Juvenile

Description: 9.5". Plump-looking sandpiper with **relatively short, straight bill**, narrow white wing stripe, and **pale gray tail** in flight. BREEDING: Upperparts gray, black, and rufous checkered, **underparts entirely rufous** except white undertail; legs black. NONBREEDING: Plain gray-brown above, white below, speckled breast; legs greenish. JUVENILE: Like nonbreeding but fine pale feather edgings above.

Similar Species: Much shorter-billed than dowitchers (page 189). In breeding plumage, rufous below contrasts with mostly gray back and white undertail, unlike dowitchers, which look all rusty-brown. Sanderling (page 179) similar-shaped but much smaller.

Status and Habitat: Common spring (May), uncommon fall (August–September) migrant on ocean beaches and mudflats, mostly on outer coast. Bottle Beach State Park on south side of Grays Harbor best place in spring. Much less common in protected waters, rarely on fresh water.

Behavior: Moves steadily, probing for invertebrates in wet mud covered by water or not. Can be in large flocks in spring, often associated with Short-billed Dowitchers and Black-bellied Plovers. More likely to be scattered individuals in fall.

Voice: Mostly silent, occasionally soft *cur-ret* in flight.

Did you know? The knots on our coast in spring are probably on their way to Siberia from western Mexico, although the migration route is not well known.

Date & Location Seen: _____

Breeding

Nonbreeding

Description: 10". Dark, **stocky sandpiper**, with **short, broad-based bill** (black with yellow base), broad white wing stripe, **white tail with broad black band at tip**, and short yellow legs. BREEDING: Bright rufous markings on scapular feathers (fade to peach in returning migrants); heavily marked with dark chevrons on white belly. NONBREEDING: Evenly gray-brown with gray chevrons on sides. JUVENILE: Like nonbreeding but with fine white feather edges on back and wing coverts.

Similar Species: Black Turnstone (page 173) smaller and darker, with white on back and wing base visible in flight. All other sandpipers have longer bills. Feeds by steadily advancing, unlike plovers (with similarly short bills) that run and stop.

Status and Habitat: Fairly common winter resident along outer coast and locally through protected waters (mid July–April). Rocky and gravel shores, jetties, and breakwaters. Good spots include Penn Cove, Alki Point, and the jetties at Grays Harbor.

Behavior: Forages by pulling mussels, barnacles, and other marine invertebrates from rocks. Roosts and feeds in flocks, almost always with other rock-loving shorebirds, particularly Black Turnstones. Often allows close approach.

Voice: Seldom vocal in region; occasional high-pitched notes or chattering.

Did you know? The nesting grounds of the Surfbird on remote Alaska ridges remained undiscovered until the 1920s.

Date & Location Seen: _____

Breeding

Nonbreeding

Description: 7.5". **Small sandpiper** with black, relatively short, **straight, blunt-tipped bill**, and **short black legs**. In flight, broad **white wing stripe** contrasts with dark flight feathers. BREEDING: Upperparts and breast **rufous**, underparts white. NON-BREEDING: **Very pale brownish gray above** with clean white underparts. JUVENILE: Upperparts more spangled with blackish above, may show some buff on breast.

Similar Species: Other small sandpipers darker than Sanderling in nonbreeding plumage. Bright rufous breeding plumage unique (seen only late spring).

Status and Habitat: Fairly common migrant and winter resident (August–May). Still some birds going north in early June. Abundant on outer coast, less common in protected waters and on mudflats, rarely on fresh water. Large numbers on ocean beaches at Ocean Shores and Westport, many at Dungeness.

Behavior: Actively forages on beach just above waves, looks like windup toy while running back and forth with legs moving rapidly. Picks and probes for small worms and crustaceans on sand or mud. Roosts and feeds in flocks, often with Dunlins.

Voice: Most common call sharp *kip*.

Did you know? Sanderlings that winter in the southern hemisphere may fly over 8,000 miles each spring to reach their high-arctic nesting grounds.

Date & Location Seen: _____

Breeding

Nonbreeding

Description: 8.25". Fairly small, **hunched appearance**, with **long bill with drooping tip**, short black legs; white wing stripe visible in flight. BREEDING: Spring birds mostly **rufous above** with whitish, heavily streaked head and breast and **black belly patch**. NONBREEDING: **Plain brownish gray back and breast**, white belly, faint eye-line.

Similar Species: Larger with longer bill than Least (page 185) and Western (page 187) Sandpipers. Smaller size and shorter, drooping bill separate Dunlin from dowitchers (page 189).

Status and Habitat: Common migrant and winter resident in region, arrives late in fall (October). Attains breeding plumage by mid April, departs by early May, when in huge flocks with dowitchers and Western Sandpipers. Wintering flocks number in tens of thousands at bays in protected waters, also abundant on outer coast. Bays, tidal flats, muddy fields, rarely far from salt water.

Behavior: Forages by probing in mud for amphipods, snails and other invertebrates. Tight, swirling flocks move with mechanized precision, alternately flashing white and brown; large numbers in distance may appear to be drifting smoke.

Voice: Flight call harsh *cheezp*.

Did you know? Formerly known as Red-backed Sandpiper in reference to its bright spring color, the Dunlin derives its current name from the "dun" plumage it wears for most of the year.

Date & Location Seen: _____

Baird's Sandpiper
Juvenile

Pectoral Sandpiper
Juvenile

Description: 7". Small sandpiper with straight, slender bill, buffy breast, **buff-scaled back** (juveniles in fall); **long wings, black legs.** BREEDING: Back mottled with black. **Similar Species**: Western (page 187) and Least (page 185) Sandpipers smaller, shorter-winged. Pectoral (below) a bit larger and darker, with more prominently striped breast, yellow legs. **Status and Habitat:** Uncommon fall migrant, July–September, almost all juveniles. Margins of freshwater ponds and edges of mudflats on salt water. **Behavior**: Forages rapidly, picking invertebrates at or above water's edge, rarely in water. Usually single or in flocks of similar species. **Voice**: Rolling *prreeet*, usually in flight. **Did you know?** Baird's is the most likely small sandpiper on alpine lakes.

Description: 8-8.5" Male perceptibly larger than female. Long-winged brown sandpiper with **sharp demarcation** between brown breast and white belly, rufous and white streaks above; **yellow legs.** BREEDING: Plainer brown above. **Similar Species**: Baird's (above) smaller, buffier, black-legged. **Status and Habitat**: Uncommon fall migrant, July–October, in both fresh and salt marshes. Rarely also in spring (May). **Behavior**: Usually forages among marsh vegetation, picking insects and other invertebrates from leaves and mud. **Voice**: Rolling *prreet*, louder than Baird's. **Did you know?** Male Pectorals attract females with flight display and mate with them, but female then carries out all parental care.

Date & Location Seen: _____

Breeding

Nonbreeding

Description: 5.5". **Smallest sandpiper**, brownish above with speckled **brownish breast** and white belly. **Short, slightly drooping bill** and yellow legs. Narrow white wing stripe visible in flight. BREEDING: Darker, with black centers on rufous back feathers, white lines down back. NONBREEDING: Evenly grayish brown above. JUVENILE : More rufous than breeding adult, fine lines on buffy breast.

Similar Species: Western Sandpiper (page 149) and Baird's Sandpiper (page 183) have black legs. Baird's larger, buffy, with thin, straight bill. Pectoral Sandpiper (page 183) similar but much larger, wings and legs proportionally longer.

Status and Habitat: Common migrant throughout lowlands, April–May and July–October; a few winter. Equally common at fresh and salt water, on mudflats of bays and estuaries, pond margins, and marshes.

Behavior: Forages mostly by picking, sometimes probing, for insects and other aquatic invertebrates. Typically forages at upper edge of mudflats and in vegetation still higher up. Frequently in small groups rather than large flocks. Not shy, often allowing close approach.

Voice: Flight call *pree eet*. Birds may utter *dee dee dee* call among themselves.

Did you know? The small North American sandpipers (including Least and Western) are often referred to collectively as "peeps," all closely related to the stints of Eurasia.

Date & Location Seen: _____

Breeding

Juvenile

WESTERN SANDPIPER
Calidris mauri

Description: 6.5". Small sandpiper, brownish gray above and white below with evenly tapered, **drooping, fine-tipped bill**, pale eye-line, and **black legs.** Narrow white wing stripe visible in flight. BREEDING: **Much rufous on head and back**, dark chevrons on flanks. NONBREEDING: Grayish above with white underparts. JUVENILE: Lacks rufous on head and markings on sides of breeding adult.

Similar Species: Semipalmated Sandpiper (rare migrant) has blunt, short bill, little or no rufous coloring. Baird's Sandpiper (page 183) slightly larger with thin, straight bill, folded wings extend well beyond tail. Sanderling (page 179) larger, with shorter, blunt bill. Least Sandpiper (page 185) has yellowish legs, is more brownish, especially breast, in all plumages.

Status and Habitat: Common migrant in coastal areas and scattered inland (April–May, July–October; a few winter). Larger flocks in spring than fall. Inhabits beaches and mudflats of tidal estuaries as well as ponds and flooded fields.

Behavior: Probes and picks tiny invertebrates from mud while wading or walking. Feeds and roosts in flocks with other shorebirds.

Voice: Flight call thin *dzheet*. Feeding flocks may chatter.

Did you know? Western Sandpiper is the most abundant migrant shorebird in western Washington. Spring counts at Grays Harbor have totaled hundreds of thousands in a day!

Date & Location Seen: _____

Short-billed Dowitcher Breeding

Short-billed Dowitcher Juvenile

Long-billed Dowitcher Breeding

Long-billed Dowitcher Juvenile

Description: 10.5". Medium-sized sandpipers with **long straight bill**, pale line over eye, finely barred tail, greenish legs, mostly dark wings, **white wedge on back** in flight. BREEDING: Dark upperparts with complex pale markings, **rusty underparts**. NONBREEDING: Overall grayish. JUVENILE: Patterned brown above, buffy breast. **Short-billed** breeding plumage with dark dots at sides of breast, much white on belly. Juvenile with **rufous-patterned tertials** (inner wing feathers covering tip of folded wing). **Long-billed** breeding plumage with underparts entirely rusty, dark bars at sides of breast. Juvenile with plain tertials.

Similar Species: Longer bill than similar-sized shorebirds except Wilson's Snipe (page 191), which has white stripes on crown and back.

Status and Habitat: Fairly common migrants throughout lowlands, peaking in May. In fall **Short-billed** arrives late June, departs September. **Long-billed** arrives July, common into October, a few winter. Both widespread, but **Short-billed** prefers tideflats, **Long-billed** fresh water.

Behavior: With head down, probe mud rapidly like sewing machine for burrowing invertebrates. Usually in flocks, often with other shorebirds.

Voice: **Short-billed** low, liquid, whistled *tu tu tu*, given in flight. **Long-billed** sharp *keek*, sometimes in rapid series.

Did you know? The two species can be difficult to distinguish. Bill length averages longer for Long-billed, but there is much overlap.

Date & Location Seen: _____

Description: 10.5″. Mostly brown plump-looking sandpiper with **long straight bill**. Bold brown and white stripes on head, **white stripes on back**, white below with heavily barred flanks. Short orange tail, greenish legs. Wings dark above and below in flight.

Similar Species: Much longer bill than other similar-sized shorebirds except dowitchers (page 83), which lack white stripe on crown and white stripes on back.

Status and Habitat: Fairly common migrant and winter resident (September–May) throughout lowlands, up to moderate elevations; uncommon breeder. Wet ground including marshes, bogs, and flooded fields.

Behavior: Forages mostly for insects, worms, and other invertebrates by probing mud and shallow water. Sits tight, relying on camouflage until approached closely, then flushes explosively, often flying high and away. May be in loose flocks during migration. Male flies high in breeding display, with shallow dives during which vibrating tail feathers produce hollow sound with Doppler effect ("winnowing").

Voice: Abrupt rasping *skaip* uttered when flushed. Breeding call *chipa chipa chipa*, repeated many times from exposed perch.

Did you know? The eyes of the Wilson's Snipe are set well back on the sides of the head, enabling it literally to watch its back for danger even as it probes for food.

Date & Location Seen: _____

Breeding Female

Nonbreeding

Description: 8.5″. **Thin-billed, often swimming sandpiper**; short legs with lobed toes. Plain wings and whitish tail in flight. BREEDING: Gray crown and back, black neck stripe shading into rufous on back, another rufous stripe on wings, white below; black legs. Male duller. NONBREEDING: Entirely gray above with white stripe above eye, white below; greenish legs. JUVENILE: Like nonbreeding but browner, buff-striped upperparts.

Similar Species: Other two phalaropes (page 195) more likely at sea, have vivid black eye-stripes in nonbreeding plumage and conspicuous white wing stripes in flight. Yellowlegs (page 167) with similar flight pattern but darker, long legs projecting behind tail.

Status and Habitat: Uncommon migrant (May and August) in freshwater marshes in lowlands, rarely on salt water in estuaries. Has bred at several lowland localities but not regularly.

Behavior: Usually seen swimming but often walks or runs in shallow water or on shore; looks awkward on land. Picks small insects and crustaceans from near surface. Females court males and lay eggs in nests constructed by their mate, who then incubates eggs and cares for young.

Voice: Nasal *ernt* calls frequently heard on breeding grounds.

Did you know? Wilson's Phalaropes winter primarily on high-altitude alkaline lakes in South America, habitats they share with flamingos.

Date & Location Seen: _____

**Red-necked Phalarope
Breeding Female**

**Red-necked Phalarope
Juvenile**

**Red Phalarope
Breeding Female**

**Red Phalarope
Nonbreeding**

Description: 7" / 7.5". **Swimming sandpipers** with **black hind cap and line behind eye** in fall; short legs with lobed toes. Both with prominent white wing stripe. **Red-necked** with thin black bill. BREEDING: Female with gray cap, white chin, reddish neck, gold-striped back, gray sides, white belly. Male similar but duller. NONBREEDING: Gray and white striped above, white below. **Red** larger, with shorter, thicker bill. BREEDING: Female with gray cap, white cheeks, rufous underparts, yellow bill. Male duller. NONBREEDING: Like Red-necked but with unstriped gray back. JUVENILES of both striped black and buff above.

Similar Species: Breeding Wilson's Phalarope (page 85) dark stripe extends from bill down side of neck, no wing stripe; nonbreeding with no black eye stripe, plain wings.

Status and Habitat: Both fairly common fall migrants on open water, late July–October (**Red** extends into early winter); less common spring migrants, mostly May. **Red** more restricted to open ocean and **Red-necked** more widespread on smaller water bodies, both uncommon on fresh water.

Behavior: Flocks swim on open water, often in circles, picking small organisms from surface.

Voice: Frequent sharp notes, like *kit kit kit*.

Did you know? Sexual roles are reversed in phalaropes, with smaller, duller-plumaged males incubating the eggs and raising the young.

Date & Location Seen: _____

Adult

Description: 20″, wingspan 40″. Fast-flying gull-like bird, **wings dark above and below**, with **white flashes** toward tips. Elongate **pointed central tail feathers**. LIGHT MORPH: Brown above, mostly white below, dark brown cap and undertail coverts. DARK MORPH: Entirely dark brown. JUVENILE: Barred and mottled brown all over, only short point on tail. Transition to adult plumage probably over three years.

Similar Species: Easily distinguished from gulls by white flash in dark wings, different color pattern.

Status and Habitat: Uncommon spring and fall migrant on outer coast and protected waters. Seen from shore but travels far out over ocean as well. More common in fall but less common than previously because of decline in Common Terns.

Behavior: Often rest on water, then fly with blinding speed toward smaller bird (typically Bonaparte's Gull or Common Tern) that has caught a fish and pursues it until it drops it. If the luckless smaller bird doesn't do so immediately, the jaeger will grab it by wing or tail and swing it around. This is kleptoparasitism at its most exciting.

Voice: Silent away from breeding grounds.

Did you know? Jaegers feed largely by kleptoparasitism when over the ocean in migration but are predators on lemmings and birds on their tundra breeding grounds.

Date & Location Seen: _____

_____

Breeding

Nonbreeding

COMMON MURRE
Uria aalge

Description: 17". In all plumages, **back and crown black** (dark brown in good light), **breast and underparts white; bill long, straight, black.** BREEDING: Entire head and neck black (some hold plumage during winter). NONBREEDING, IMMATURE: Throat and neck mostly white, with **dark line behind eye**. Shaped like football in flight.

Similar Species: Large size, solid dark back and upperwing, and long bill separate it from nonbreeding Marbled (page 203) and Ancient (page 205) Murrelets and Pigeon Guillemot (page 201).

Status and Habitat: Fairly common winter resident on marine waters; abundance varies year to year. Nests on steep seaside cliffs on outer coast north of Grays Harbor. Many birds winter at sea but also common in protected waters with strong tidal flow. Good places include Dungeness Spit, Cattle Point, Port Townsend, and viewpoints on outer coast.

Behavior: Dives for schooling fish and squids. Congregates at good feeding sites. Flies in lines, sometimes with Rhinoceros Auklets.

Voice: Males take single young to sea in late summer, call *murr, murr*, and young answers with high-pitched cries.

Did you know? Common Murres routinely dive to 200 feet, propelling themselves with small wings adapted for underwater swimming. In the air, however, they must beat their wings in a rapid blur to keep their two-pound bodies aloft.

Date & Location Seen: _____

Breeding

Nonbreeding

Description: 13". Medium-small alcid with slender black bill; **legs and mouth lining vermilion red**. BREEDING: **Blackish** except upper surface of forewing largely white; when wing folded, appears as **large white patch** with black slash on lower edge. NON-BREEDING: **Looks pale**, white finely mottled with black, dark line through eye; white wing patch retained. JUVENILE: Resembles nonbreeding adult, but duskier, dark-capped, often little white in wing. Two years to maturity.

Similar Species: In flight, White-winged Scoter (page 65) shows white patches on trailing edge of wing; Pigeon Guillemot's white patch is on forewing. Guillemots and other alcids look short-necked in comparison with other diving birds.

Status and Habitat: Fairly common year-round resident, widely distributed on marine waters. In winter, concentrates in good feeding areas (Tacoma Narrows, Budd Inlet, Sequim Bay, Rosario Strait, Grays Harbor). Nests in crevices along shoreline, including on breakwaters, jetties and piers, majority in burrows in bluffs. Forages in relatively shallow protected waters.

Behavior: Takes small fish, shrimp, and crabs by diving to bottom, using both wings and feet for propulsion.

Voice: High-pitched trills and whistles given during breeding season.

Did you know? Winter numbers increase in the region as Pigeon Guillemots move north from California and abandon the outer coast.

Date & Location Seen: _____

201

Breeding

Nonbreeding

Description: 9″. **Small**, short-necked alcid with **slender black bill.** BREEDING: **Dark brown, "marbled" with buff.** NONBREEDING: Black above, white below, **white stripe** on either side of back. White throat and collar give bird **black-capped** look. Wings narrower and more pointed than other alcids in region.

Similar Species: Ancient Murrelet (page 205) same size as Marbled, with yellow bill, gray back contrasting with black head, no white back stripes. Underwing white (dark in Marbled).

Status and Habitat: Uncommon year-round resident in region; in winter usually seen in pairs. Forages in relatively shallow saltwater bays, inlets and passages, especially north (Admiralty Inlet, Rosario Strait, San Juan Islands); also Grays Harbor. Nests in old-growth forests near coast, commuting to salt water to forage; winters on protected marine waters. Populations seriously declining.

Behavior: Dives for small fish and crustaceans. Flies with rapid wingbeats, looking like big sea-going bee.

Voice: Call loud, high-pitched *keer keer keer*, so members of pair can locate one another after diving.

Did you know? The first Marbled Murrelet nest was discovered only in 1974. Nests are high in large conifers, very difficult to see. With continued logging of old-growth forests, the species has undergone a 90% decline in numbers in our region in historic times.

Date & Location Seen: _____

Ancient Murrelet
Nonbreeding

Cassin's Auklet
Adult

Description: 9″. Small alcid, **gray and black above** and white below. Mostly **black head** contrasts with gray back; **bill yellowish**. Underwings white. **Similar Species**: Marbled Murrelet black above with two white stripes on back, dark underwings, most often in pairs. **Status and Habitat**: Uncommon winter resident, arriving in protected waters in November, all the way to southern Puget Sound, then disappearing out to sea by midwinter. **Behavior**: Forages for fish in deep water. Often in small flocks flying rapidly over water that suddenly dive under while in flight. Pop up, regroup and take off again. **Voice**: Silent in winter. **Did you know?** From island nesting burrows, half-grown young head out to sea accompanied by parents.

CASSIN'S AUKLET *Ptychoramphus aleuticus*

Description: 8″. Small alcid, dark **gray-brown** above and white below with **short, thick bill**, white eye crescents. **Similar Species**: Murrelets (above, page 203) slender-billed, black and white or all dark brown. **Status and Habitat**: Common breeder on outer coast islands, forages and winters out at sea; rare visitor to protected waters. **Behavior**: Nests in burrows on islands, flies well offshore to forage. At colony only at night to avoid predatory gulls. Feeds on planktonic crustaceans and larval fish. **Voice**: Noisy at breeding colony, silent at sea. **Did you know?** Cassin's Auklets store a wad of prey in a throat pouch for the long flight back to the nest.

Date & Location Seen: _____

Rhinoceros Auklet
Breeding

Tufted Puffin
Breeding

Description: 13". **Dark gray-brown** alcid; light belly visible in flight. **Large yellow-orange bill** (smaller and dark in juveniles). BREEDING: **White plumes** behind eye and bill; short "horn" at base of upper bill. **Similar Species**: Breeding Marbled Murrelet (page 183) much smaller, slender-billed, with dark belly. Immature Tufted Puffin (below) similar in coloration, but larger with huge bill. **Status and Habitat:** Common coastal resident (huge colony on Protection Island), April–September. Much less common in winter; majority winter at sea. **Behavior**: Dives for fish in deep water. Often forages in tide rips. Nests colonially, visiting nests at night. **Voice**: Silent away from nests. **Did you know?** Pairs excavate nest burrows to 15 feet deep on grassy slopes.

TUFTED PUFFIN *Fratercula cirrhata*

Description: 15". **Blackish** alcid with **compressed orange bill**. BREEDING: Face white, **long yellow tufts** back from eyes. NONBREEDING: All dark with brown bill base. IMMATURE: Smaller, darker bill. **Similar Species**: Male Surf Scoter (page 63) only vaguely similar. Immature could be mistaken for Rhinoceros Auklet (above). **Status and Habitat:** Fairly common breeder on outer coast islands from Seal Island to Grenville Rocks, also small populations on Smith and Protection Islands. Winters at sea. **Behavior**: Dives deep for fish, carries multiple individuals back to nest. Nests in rock crevices or burrows on grassy hillsides. **Voice**: Silent away from breeding island. **Did you know?** Puffins and other members of the family Alcidae are called "alcids."

Date & Location Seen:

Breeding

Description: 17", wingspan 38". Smallish gull, white with **short yellow bill** and **black legs**, pale gray back with **narrowly black wingtips.** Tail slightly notched. NONBREEDING: Dark hindneck collar. JUVENILE: Like nonbreeding but blackish M-shaped marking across entire wings, black tail tip.

Similar Species: Mew Gull (page 215), another small gull with entirely yellow bill, has white in wingtips and yellow legs; not offshore.

Status and Habitat: Uncommon winter visitor (September–May) on open ocean off outer coast, sometimes seen from shore. Much more rarely penetrates into Strait of Juan de Fuca. Formerly common, even through summer, but substantial recent decline. Large numbers only rarely seen now, usually well offshore.

Behavior: Forages on small schooling fish and planktonic crustaceans at ocean surface by plunge-diving. When not over ocean, roosts on jetties and occasionally beaches. Distinctive choppy wingbeat.

Voice: Loud, repeated *kit-i-wak* on breeding grounds, silent away from them.

Did you know? Kittiwakes are the only cliff-nesting gull in North America. Huge colonies of them breed on Alaskan islands. The species has undergone substantial population declines in recent decades, perhaps because of effects of global climate change on their prey species.

Date & Location Seen: _____

Bonaparte's Gull
Nonbreeding

Franklin's Gull
Immature

Description: 13.5", wingspan 29". **Petite**, tern-like in flight. White with pearl-gray back, black bill, and short red legs. **Front part of wing white** beyond wrist, trailing edge black. BREEDING: **Head black**. NONBREEDING: **Head white with black spot behind eye**. IMMATURE: Rear edge of wing and tail tip black. Matures in second year.

Similar Species: Immature **Franklin's Gull**, *Leucophaeus pipixcan*, larger, with darker brownish gray upperparts and black hood on back of head. Common Tern (page 229) has strongly forked tail, black limited to cap.

Status and Habitat: Common migrant (March–May, August–October), smaller numbers in winter. Mostly in protected coastal waters, fewer on outer coast; regular at sewage lagoons. **Franklin's** rare, usually in fall (August–October) and often at sewage ponds with Bonaparte's.

Behavior: Forages for small fish and crustaceans by plunge-diving or picking at water surface. Concentrates, occasionally in flocks of hundreds, at tidal rips and sewage ponds. Flocks move together over open water to search for feeding opportunities.

Voice: Calls unlike those of most gulls—low, harsh, grating *geerr*.

Did you know? Bonaparte's Gulls build their nests in conifers in the boreal forests of Alaska and Canada. Franklin's Gulls nest in the Great Plains and migrate south to the Humboldt Current off Peru and Chile.

Date & Location Seen: _____

Nonbreeding

Immature

Description: 18", wingspan 46". Medium-sized **dark gray** gull with **red bill**, light gray rump and underparts, **black tail with white tip**. BREEDING: White head. NONBREEDING: Head gray. JUVENILE: Uniform dark brown with pinkish, black-tipped bill. Transition to adult plumage over three years.

Similar Species: Distinctive in region. Other adult gulls white below, immatures streaked or mottled. Parasitic Jaeger (page 197) falcon-like; plumage variable but always with white flash near wing tip. Tiny percentage of Heermann's Gulls have white patch at wing bend.

Status and Habitat: Fairly common summer visitor (June–October) after breeding in Gulf of California, few staying into winter recently; absent in spring. Strictly coastal, shuns fresh water. Common on outer coast and through San Juan Islands, less so farther south. Big roost at Edmonds breakwater.

Behavior: Forages in flight over water for fish and small invertebrates; picks from surface or makes shallow dives. Prefers to roost on rocks, sometimes in large, dense groups set apart from other gulls.

Voice: Calls more nasal and hollow than those of other gulls.

Did you know? These gulls accompany Brown Pelicans north to our waters and try to steal fish from them. Most gulls are kleptoparasites, attempting to take prey from other individuals, but not so specifically oriented as this species.

Date & Location Seen: _____

Nonbreeding

Immature

Description: 16.5", wingspan 38". Small white gull with light slaty gray back and wings, **dove-like head, dark eye, short yellowish bill**, yellow legs. Wingtips black with **large white spot at tip**. NONBREEDING: Head heavily mottled. FIRST YEAR: Coffee and cream color with darker wing and tail. Adult plumage attained in three years. Second-year bird resembles adult but with black tail tip, ring near end of bill.

Similar Species: Smaller than most gulls in region. Darker gray above, more white in wingtips than Ring-billed (page 217).

Status and Habitat: Common winter resident (August–May) in coastal areas. Commonest winter gull in Puget Sound along with Glaucous-winged. Can be anywhere on salt water, also at lakes and up rivers near coast.

Behavior: Takes small fish and invertebrates by hovering with feet dangling in water at tidal rips (convergence lines) in deeper water. Also forages for worms in plowed fields and, like many other species, for water bugs in sewage ponds. May flycatch during insect hatches. Often roosts with shorebirds and other gulls but stays clear of large species.

Voice: Calls higher than those of other gulls, with mewing quality.

Did you know? Although it nests on Vancouver Island at the door of the Puget Sound Region, there are no breeding records of Mew Gull in Washington.

Date & Location Seen: _____

Nonbreeding

Immature

Description: 17.5", wingspan 46". **Medium-sized** gull, white with pearl-gray back and wings; **wingtips extensively black** with white spots at tip. **Yellow bill with black ring near tip**, yellow eye and legs. NONBREEDING: Head streaked. FIRST YEAR: Pale gray and white with brown markings, dark band at tail tip, dark eye, pink-based bill and pink legs. Transition to adult plumage over three years.

Similar Species: Larger gulls have heavier bills. California Gull (page 219) darker above. Mew Gull (page 215) darker above, whiter wingtips, and smaller bill without ring.

Status and Habitat: Common resident, although very local as breeder, perhaps only Grays Harbor at present. Throughout lowlands, rare at higher elevations. More common at fresh water than other gulls, often on agricultural fields and in urban settings.

Behavior: Forages widely for worms in plowed fields and fish in coastal areas; also refuse and scraps in cities. Often flycatches during termite hatches. Like other gulls, long-lived colonial nester with elaborate courtship and complex social behavior. Gregarious, often flocks with other gulls.

Voice: Typical gull calls (harsher than larger species) include long sequence of laugh-like squeals, beginning with long calls then trailing to shorter ones.

Did you know? Other gull species have rings on their bills during immaturity. Take care not to confuse them with Ring-billed Gulls.

Date & Location Seen: _____

_____

Nonbreeding

Immature

Description: 19", wingspan 50". Medium–large gull. White with **slaty gray back, black wingtips** with white spots at tip. Dark eye, fairly slender **bill with black and red spot, greenish legs.** NONBREEDING: Head streaked. FIRST YEAR: Brown, variably dark, with darker wingtips and tail; black-tipped pink bill and pink legs. Transition to full adult plumage over four years.

Similar Species: Only adult gull in region with greenish legs, black and red spot on bill. Smaller than Herring and Thayer's (page 221), larger than Ring-billed (page 217), darker back than any of them also readily seen from below.

Status and Habitat: Uncommon winter–spring in region, becomes fairly common by late July, most common gull on coast late summer–fall as migrants arrive from breeding colonies to east and north. Primarily lowlands and mostly coastal, but may be seen flying west over mountain passes in summer.

Behavior: Forages in coastal areas for fish and invertebrates, including far out into ocean; also in plowed fields for rodents and worms and in cities for refuse. May flycatch or steal food from other birds. Often flocks with other gulls.

Voice: Typical for gull but harsher than larger species.

Did you know? California Gulls rescued Mormon settlers at Great Salt Lake from the "locust" (Mormon cricket) plague of 1848.

Date & Location Seen: _____

Herring Gull
Nonbreeding

Thayer's Gull
Nonbreeding

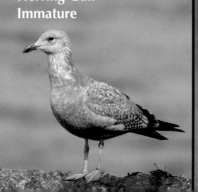

Herring Gull
Immature

Thayer's Gull
Immature

HERRING GULL / THAYER'S (ICELAND) GULL
Larus argentatus / Larus glaucoides thayeri

Description: 21" / 20", wingspan 54" / 52". Large gulls with **light gray back** and wings and **dark wingtips**, otherwise white; **yellow bill with red spot, pink legs.** Adult **Herring** eye always yellow. **Thayer's** slightly smaller, with round head, distinctly **smaller bill** and typically **dark eye**, less often yellowish. **Herring** with black wingtips above and below. **Thayer's** wingtips with less black and more white, **much paler below than above.** NONBREEDING: Dusky streaks on head. FIRST YEAR: Variably mottled brown with darker wings and tail, bill black. Transition to full adult plumage over four years. Thayer's is now considered a subspecies of Iceland Gull.

Similar Species: Adult California (page 219) and Ring-billed (page 217) Gulls have greenish or yellow legs, more black on wingtips. Hybrid Glaucous-winged x Western Gulls (page 225) somewhat similar but bill heavier, wingtip color varies along with back color.

Status and Habitat: Both fairly common winter residents (October–April), mostly in coastal areas but on both fresh and salt water. Look in mixed gull flocks anywhere. **Herring** more widespread inland.

Behavior: Forage mostly for fish, crabs, mollusks, carrion, and urban refuse. Gregarious, often flocking with other gulls.

Voice: Typical gull cries.

Did you know? These and many other gulls come well up the Lower Columbia River in early spring to feed on the smelt that spawn there.

Date & Location Seen: _____

Breeding

Immature

Description: 21", wingspan 54". Large gull, white with **dark gray back** and **black wingtips. Massive bill yellow with red spot, eye yellowish**, legs pink. JUVENILE: Medium brown and heavily mottled, wings and tail darker. Bill black, eye dark. Transition to adult plumage over four years.

Similar Species: Other large common gulls all have paler gray backs. Western has thickest bill of any. Hybridizes with Glaucous-winged Gull (page 225), producing birds intermediate in back and wingtip color.

Status and Habitat: Common resident on outer coast, smaller numbers into Strait of Juan de Fuca and down into Puget Sound, especially in winter. Many Western-like gulls in Puget Sound could be hybrids. Occurs from shore to well offshore out of sight of land. Normally marine, but a few wander up Lower Columbia River and visit coastal lakes.

Behavior: Forages at shore and on water for fish and just about anything else it can subdue, also carrion and refuse. Visits fish-processing plants and boats to get castoffs. Breeds in large numbers on rocky and sandy islands.

Voice: Typical loud gull calls, longer and more complex during breeding interactions.

Did you know? Gulls live long lives, up to 30-40 years, and mate for life but will rapidly remate if original mate lost.

Date & Location Seen: _____

Nonbreeding

Immature

Description: 21", wingspan 54". Large gull, white with pearl-gray back and wings, **wingtips only slightly darker than back**, white spots near tip. **Large yellow bill with red spot** near tip, eye brown, legs pink. NONBREEDING: Head mottled. FIRST YEAR: Coffee with cream color all over, including wings and tail. Transition to full adult plumage over four years.

Similar Species: Most gulls smaller with smaller bills; other large gulls have black wingtips, except Glaucous Gull (rare in region) with white wingtips.

Status and Habitat: Common coastal resident throughout marine habitats, including rocky shores and beaches and well out to sea. Also inland as nonbreeder up larger rivers and around urban lakes.

Behavior: Omnivorous and opportunistic. Forages on land and water for fish, invertebrates, and carrion in coastal areas, refuse in cities, and worms in fields. Persistent kleptoparasite, chasing other birds, including its own species, to steal prey items. Nests in pairs on islands, pilings, roofs, and other structures. Gregarious, flocking with other gulls.

Voice: Calls, typical for gull, include sequences of laugh-like bugling, staccato *ca ca ca* given in alarm.

Did you know? Glaucous-winged Gull freely hybridizes with the more southerly Western Gull, and the resulting offspring are intermediate in plumage. Many "glaucous-wings" in the Puget Sound Region are actually hybrids.

Date & Location Seen: _____

Breeding

Breeding

Description: 20", wingspan 48". Stocky tern, pearl-gray above and white below, with **thick, pointed red bill, black cap**, and shallowly forked tail; **long, pointed wings** with tips dark on underside. NONBREEDING: Whitish forehead. JUVENILE: Like nonbreeding but back mottled with brown.

Similar Species: Common Tern (page 229) much smaller, slender bill. Except for Heermann's (page 213), gulls lack red bill, and no gull has wingtips white above and dark below.

Status and Habitat: Fairly common summer resident (April–September) along entire coast but breeding very local, possibly now only on Sand Island in Lower Columbia. Colonies in protected waters mostly abandoned but wandering birds seen widely. Usually colonial nester on open sites, including recently disturbed ground, dredge-spoil islands, even rooftops.

Behavior: Flies fairly high over salt or fresh water, plunge-dives for small fish, often well below surface; also picks fish off surface. Carries fish in bill back to nest. Colony locations may shift year to year depending on disturbance.

Voice: Often heard before seen. Common call loud, harsh, protracted *rrrau*. Juveniles beg with whistled *wheee oo*.

Did you know? Because they capture salmon smolts swimming downriver from hatcheries, Caspian Terns have come into increasing conflict with fisheries management goals, and several of their colonies have been purposely broken up by agencies and tribes.

Date & Location Seen: _____

Breeding

Breeding

COMMON TERN
Sterna hirundo

Description: 13.5", wingspan 29". **Slim, elegant,** pearl-gray above and white below with **black cap,** thin, black-tipped red bill, and short, red-orange legs. **Tail strongly forked,** white with dark edges; **wings long, pointed** with dark tips on under surface of outer wing feathers (primaries), also dark wedge on upper surface in fall. NONBREEDING: Black bill, white forehead. JUVENILE: Like nonbreeding but dark bar on leading edge of inner wing.

Similar Species: Caspian Tern (page 227) much larger with thick bill. Bonaparte's Gull (page 211) has black head and bill in spring, square tail, mostly white forewing.

Status and Habitat: Formerly fairly common migrant, mostly late summer–fall. Locally on marine waters everywhere, open coast to Puget Sound, but sharp decline in recent years, so now somewhat difficult to find. Often concentrates near tidal rips and roosts on beaches and pilings.

Behavior: Forages for small fish by flying low over water, hovering, and plunge-diving to catch prey with bill. Gregarious, sometimes flocking with small gulls and Caspian Terns.

Voice: Calls include clipped *kip* and harsh but musical, slurred *kee ahrr.*

Did you know? The breeding and winter ranges of this species are both to the east of Washington, and their decline here may be no more than a shift in their migration route.

Date & Location Seen: _____

ROCK PIGEON
Columba livia

Description: 13". Familiar **domestic pigeon** with dark bill, short reddish legs. **Highly variable in color and pattern**, from black to white. Common form (original coloration) pale gray with darker gray head and neck, iridescent green on neck, two black bars across wing, **black band at tail tip**. Many birds darker and more heavily marked, others with much white, others peach-colored. **White rump and underwing** visible in flight except in entirely dark birds.

Similar Species: Band-tailed Pigeon (page 233) has mostly yellow bill, white hind collar on neck, narrow dark band on middle of gray tail, yellow legs, and dark underwing.

Status and Habitat: Common and widespread year-round resident in lowlands. Native to Old World; domesticated birds introduced, now naturalized virtually worldwide. Inhabits city parks, streets, industrial zones, bridges, and overpasses; also rural seed fields, barns, and grain elevators.

Behavior: Forages mostly on ground for grain, seeds, grasses, and food scraps. Feeds and travels in flocks. Flies at speeds of up to 85 miles per hour—one of fastest birds in region.

Voice: Soft cooing.

Did you know? Introduced by early European settlers, the Rock Pigeon is now widespread throughout North America and one of the most abundant urban birds, building nests on window ledges, water towers, bridges, and other structures.

Date & Location Seen: _____

BAND-TAILED PIGEON
Patagioenas fasciata

Description: 14″. Overall gray with purplish head and breast, black-tipped **yellow bill, white collar** above iridescent feathers on nape (absent in juveniles), **narrow black band on tail**, and **yellow legs**. Dark underwing visible in flight.

Similar Species: Rock Pigeon (page 231) has white, not gray, rump, flesh-colored legs, dark bill, and white underwing. Varied colors are evident even in small flocks of Rock Pigeons.

Status and Habitat: Fairly common summer resident, uncommon in winter; most go south September–October, return beginning late February. Breeds in low-elevation coniferous and mixed forests; uncommon up to mountain passes. Prefers tall conifers for nesting, often in suburban neighborhoods. Postbreeders and migrants regular in mountains.

Behavior: Feeds mostly on nuts, seeds, and fruits of broadleaf trees and shrubs such as oak, cherry, elderberry, madrone, and cascara. Much attracted to seed feeders. Usually forages and travels in small flocks. When taking rapid flight, wings produce loud clapping noise. Two eggs in flimsy nest on sturdy branch high in tree.

Voice: Low, repetitive *who whooo*, sounding much like owl hoot.

Did you know? Band-tailed Pigeons make morning visits to mineral springs with nearby roosting trees, especially in summer—for example at Nisqually National Wildlife Refuge, Mud Bay, and Sumas Springs.

Date & Location Seen: _____

Eurasian Collared-Dove

Mourning Dove

Description: 12" / 11.5". **Long-tailed doves. Collared: Pale grayish brown** with **square tail, black hindneck collar. Mourning: Light brown** with **long, pointed tail,** black spots on wings; male has bluish crown, pinkish hue on breast.

Similar Species: African Collared-Dove (also called Ringed Turtle-Dove) similar to Eurasian but smaller, much paler, with white undertail; occurs as escaped cage bird. Rock and Band-tailed Pigeons (pages 231–233) larger, relatively shorter-tailed.

Status and Habitat: Collared uncommon but increasing resident. Native to Eurasia; introduced to North America. **Mourning** uncommon and local resident; many migrate south for winter. Both widespread in lowlands, shunning dense forest and urban core. Occupy grasslands (prairie, agricultural), farms, grain elevators, small woodlots, semi-rural residential tracts, and small towns.

Behavior: Diet almost exclusively seeds taken on ground, sometimes feeders. Often seen on overhead wires. Form flocks, especially in winter, at sites with plentiful food and nearby trees for sheltering and roosting.

Voice: Collared "song" *coo coo coop* (stress on second syllable). **Mourning** slow, mournful *ooo aaa ooo ooo ooo*.

Did you know? Eurasian Collared-Doves were introduced to the New World in the Bahamas in 1972, then jumped to Florida and amazingly reached Washington in 30 years. So far no evidence of competitive displacement by this invasive species.

Date & Location Seen: _____

Description: 13″, wingspan 40″. **Slim, long-legged, round-headed owl** with prominent **heart-shaped facial disc**; dark brown eyes, long pale bill. Orange-brown and gray back with pearl-gray spots, mostly white (male) or buffier (female) underparts impart **pale appearance**, especially in headlights at night. In flight, tail looks fairly long, wings appear bowed.

Similar Species: Barred Owl (page 247) bulkier, broader-winged, darker below. Short-eared Owl (page 249) has floppier flight, dark and pale wing patches.

Status and Habitat: Fairly common resident throughout lowlands, including cities. Prefers open areas for foraging, including farmland, fields, wetlands, clearcuts, and urban landscapes with buildings.

Behavior: Entirely nocturnal. Hunts from perch or in low flight, drops on prey silently. Directional hearing well-developed for locating rodents and shrews, its primary quarry, in high grass or leaf litter. Also takes some birds, insects, reptiles, and amphibians. Roosts in buildings, under bridges, or in dense conifers by day. Does not build nest; lays up to 10 eggs in dark corner of building, large nest box, cave, or tree cavity.

Voice: Varied calls include harsh, grating screech when flying over, also hissing and metallic clicking at nest.

Did you know? Owls cough up undigested hair and bones in pellets; a bunch of them on the ground is a sure sign of an owl roost.

Date & Location Seen: _____

Description: 9". **Small** but robust owl, mottled grayish or brownish, **block-headed** with **prominent ear-tufts** (sometimes held flat) and **yellow eyes**. Breast and belly streaked and finely barred.

Similar Species: Combination of small size and ear-tufts eliminates other owls.

Status and Habitat: Formerly fairly common but declining resident. Mostly lowlands and river drainages up to moderate elevation. Broadleaf and mixed woodlands, including forest edge and well-wooded parks. Often along watercourses. Not ubiquitous, often absent from suitable-looking habitat.

Behavior: Entirely nocturnal. Hunts from perches, swoops, and captures prey in talons. Favors rodents, large insects, and earthworms but will take birds, reptiles, and amphibians. Uses existing tree cavities for nest sites, sometimes perches at entrance during day. Usually responds to imitations of its calls by approaching and calling to protect territory.

Voice: Common call accelerating series of low whistles in pattern of ball bouncing, then coming to rest (notes start high and far apart, get progressively lower and closer together).

Did you know? Increased abundance of Barred Owls in western Washington may have a lot to do with the decline of Western Screech-Owls. There is no reason for big owls not to eat little owls, which are out and about at the same time.

Date & Location Seen: _____

_____

Description: 22″. Formidable owl, mottled grayish-brown, **block-headed** with **prominent ear-tufts. Yellow eyes**, black-ringed brownish facial disc, **white line across throat**, finely barred lower breast and belly.

Similar Species: Long-eared Owl (page 249) also has prominent ear-tufts but much smaller, with streaks as well as bars below. Barred and Spotted Owls (page 247) lack ear-tufts and have brown eyes.

Status and Habitat: Fairly common resident in countryside, less common in cities. Lowlands to tree line, although uncommon in dense forest. Very adaptable, occurring in woodlands, meadows, and farmlands, even large city parks.

Behavior: Hunts mostly at night, watching and listening for prey from perch, then pursuing and capturing it with sharp talons. Diet extremely varied, mostly small mammals but also birds, especially water birds, reptiles, amphibians, and fish. A hungry owl will take worms and grasshoppers! Does not build nest; uses snags, cavities, and nests of other species, especially Red-tailed Hawk. One of our earliest nesting birds, laying eggs as early as January.

Voice: Common call deep *whoo whodoo whoo who*. (5 notes from males, 8 from females). Begging young give harsh shrieks.

Did you know? Great Horned Owls are powerful, fearless hunters. They have been recorded killing and eating animals as large as Great Blue Herons and skunks.

Date & Location Seen: _____

Adult

Immature

Description: 23". **Round-headed, yellow-eyed, mostly white owl**, with varying amounts of dark barring and mottling. ADULT MALE: May be pure white. ADULT FEMALE: Variable but with more barring. IMMATURE: May have dense, dark barring and look darkish from a distance, but face always white.

Similar Species: Unmistakable, but note resemblance to white signs and bottles out in fields.

Status and Habitat: Very rare or absent in most years but periodically irrupts southward in winter (November–early April). Some years just a few, in others can reach a dozen or more at favored sites. Usually a majority are immatures. Most common in open coastal habitats, including beaches and salt marshes. Good bets are agricultural fields in Skagit and Samish Flats and Damon Point at Ocean Shores.

Behavior: Hunts mostly at dusk and dawn. Perches on ground, driftwood, jetties, fence posts, and human structures up to rooftops. On coast prefers shorebirds and seabirds, which it hunts even over water; rats and voles important away from coast.

Voice: Almost entirely silent in winter. Screams and hoots on tundra.

Did you know? Big flight years are presumed to be associated with high reproduction in Arctic, larger numbers of young, and greater dispersal south of usual winter latitudes.

Date & Location Seen: _____

Description: 6.5". **Tiny diurnal owl** with no ear-tufts, yellow eyes, and **relatively long, white-barred tail**. Rich brown above, dotted with white on head and back; white below with brown streaks. Black "false eyes" on back of head, ringed with white.

Similar Species: As an owl, can't be mistaken for any other type of bird, and unique among our owls in small size and daytime habits.

Status and Habitat: Fairly common resident in coniferous forests from sea level to tree line. Some dispersing in fall, best time to locate them by imitating their calls.

Behavior: Perches on exposed branches from low branches to treetops to watch for prey, usually small birds and mammals. Fierce hunter for its size, can take prey up to chipmunk size— prey larger than predator! Rapid swooping flight from tree to tree with audible fluttering. Nests in tree cavities or abandoned woodpecker nests.

Voice: Single tooting whistles given at intervals, sometimes accelerated into short series.

Did you know? Pygmy-Owl calling or imitations thereof are sure-fire attractants to small birds that come to mob the owl, a potential predator. With all the local birds aware of its presence, its best bet is to leave the area and hunt elsewhere.

Date & Location Seen: _____

Spotted Owl

Barred Owl

Description: 17". **Large round-headed owl** with **dark eyes**. Dark brown above with white spots, **barred and mottled** brown and white below. **Similar Species**: Barred Owl (below) paler, with streaked belly. Other large owls with ear-tufts. **Status and Habitat**: Increasingly rare resident of old-growth coniferous forests, lowlands to mountains. Lower west side of Cascades and Olympics best bets. **Behavior**: Nocturnal, less active in daytime than Barred Owl. Roosts quietly on horizontal branch of big tree. Hunts for voles on forest floor and flying squirrels in trees. **Voice**: Fairly deep *hoo hoo hoo hoooo*. **Did you know?** Listed as Threatened, Spotted Owl presence protects some old-growth forests from logging, but competition from Barred Owls is hastening its decline.

BARRED OWL *Strix varia*

Description: 19". Bulky, gray-brown, with **dark eyes. Round head** with ring-like pattern around dark-bordered facial disc. Bill yellowish. **Upperparts and upper breast barred, rest of underparts streaked. Similar Species**: Great Horned Owl (page 241) has ear-tufts and yellow eyes. Spotted Owl (above) dark brown, lacks streaks below. **Status and Habitat**: Recent arrival in region, now fairly common resident throughout. Prefers dense moist forests, even urban ones. **Behavior**: Mostly nocturnal. Hunts from perches; favors rodents, but eats many other small animals. Uses large cavities and nests of other species. Occasionally aggressive toward humans. **Voice**: Loud hoots including *who cooks for you, who cooks for you allll* sequence. **Did you know?** Barred Owls first reached Washington in 1965.

Date & Location Seen: _____

_____

Long-eared Owl

Short-eared Owl

Description: 13.5". Slender-looking owl with **long ear-tufts**. Mottled brown above, finely streaked and barred below; **rufous face**. **Similar Species**: Great Horned Owl (page 241) much larger, white horizontal line across throat. Western Screech-Owl (page 239) smaller, much shorter ear-tufts, gray face. Short-eared Owl (below) narrower wings, deeper wingbeat. **Status and Habitat**: Uncommon resident in woodland throughout lowlands, poorly known because of secretive habits. **Behavior**: Nocturnal, often roosts low in shrubbery during daytime. Feeds primarily on mice and voles. **Voice**: Males give around 30 deep hoots in a series. **Did you know?** Long-eared Owl populations often increase during high points of vole cycles, when they feed on nothing else.

Description: 13.5". **Moth-like flight in late afternoon**. Mottled above, finely streaked below. Yellow eyes, prominent facial disc. In flight long wings show **black and buff patches beyond wrist**. **Similar Species**: Slow, floppy flight and daytime activity unlike other large owls in region. **Status and Habitat**: Fairly common winter resident (October–April) in wet meadows, fallow fields, and coastal marshes; few recent breeding records. Frequent in Samish and Skagit River lowlands. **Behavior**: Hunts low over fields, mostly toward dusk. Locates voles, primary prey, by sound, often hovering before pouncing. Roosts on ground by day. **Voice**: Gives nasal barks and wheezy whistles during interactions. **Did you know?** Short-eared Owls nest on the ground, lay as many as ten eggs.

Date & Location Seen: _____

Northern Saw-whet
Owl

Boreal Owl

NORTHERN SAW-WHET OWL
Aegolius acadicus

Description: 7.5″. **Small round-headed**, yellow-eyed owl. Brown above with white wing spots, white below with brown streaking. **Fine white streaks on head. Similar Species**: Western Screech-Owl (page 239) larger, with ear-tufts (although these may be held flat). Northern Pygmy-Owl (page 245) smaller, with smaller head, long tail, typically active in daylight. See Boreal Owl (below). **Status and Habitat:** Fairly common resident in coniferous and mixed forest, sea level to mountain passes; numbers augmented in winter by migrants. **Behavior**: Rodents primary prey. Daytime roosts in dense conifers. Highly migratory. **Voice**: Calls include rhythmic tooting and *skyews*. **Did you know?** After putting out mist nets at night, bird banders discovered that Saw-whet Owls were surprisingly common.

BOREAL OWL *Aegolius funereus*

Description: 10″. **Smallish flat-headed owl** with yellow eyes and **pale bill.** Dark brown above with scattered **white spots, including on head**; brown and white streaked below. **Similar Species:** Saw-whet Owl (above) smaller, with streaks on head and dark bill. Western Screech-Owl (page 239) much grayer, with ear-tufts. **Status and Habitat**: Uncommon resident at high elevation in Cascades; best known from Sunrise area. **Behavior**: Entirely nocturnal; roosts in dense spruces during day. Active at night when hunting rodents but hard to see. **Voice**: Mellow tooting and loud *skyew* call when agitated. **Did you know?** Boreal Owls were first found in the Cascades in 1992 at Mount Rainier.

Date & Location Seen: _____

Description: 8.5", wingspan 20". **Usually seen high in flight** with **long, pointed, flexed wings** with **conspicuous broad white band** near tip. **Mottled gray-brown and black** above, finely barred brown below; short legs, relatively long tail. Appears owl-like at rest but **very small bill, legs, and feet**; wingtips extend beyond tail tip. MALE: White chin and tail band. FEMALE: Buffy chin.

Similar Species: Swallows and swifts much smaller; falcons have more direct flight, lack white wing bands.

Status and Habitat: Uncommon summer resident (late May–August). Sparse breeder in mountains and rural lowlands, formerly more common. Autumn transients, into September, seen more widely. Nests in open habitats such as forest clearings, gravelly river bars, and weedy lots. Hunts and migrates over all habitats.

Behavior: Forages aerially with erratic flight, mostly near dawn and dusk but can be active at any hour. Tiny bill opens to huge gape for catching insects. Perches lengthwise along branches. Nests on open ground, relying on camouflage. In courtship, males dive steeply from high up, producing booming sound.

Voice: Far-carrying nasal buzzy *peent* given repeatedly in flight.

Did you know? Nighthawks belong to a group of birds called goatsuckers, which are most closely related to swifts and hummingbirds.

Date & Location Seen: _____

_____

Black Swift

Vaux's Swift

Description: Black largest North American swift (6.5"), **Vaux's** smallest (4.5"). Both dark overall, usually seen foraging high overhead on **pointed, sickle-shaped wings** with **flickering wing-beats. Black: Longer, notched tail; wing-beat slower, shallower,** glides frequently. **Vaux's: Throat, breast, and rump paler** than rest of plumage (hard to spot in field); short tail tapers when closed, giving "**winged cigar**" look. **Wing-beat rapid** with only brief intervals of gliding.

Similar Species: Swallows (pages 313–321) use similar aerial foraging strategy but wing-beats not so flickering; wings proportionally shorter, broader, flexed at wrist.

Status and Habitat: Widely distributed summer residents (May–August), **Vaux's** locally fairly common but **Black** rather scarce. **Black** nests in cliff crevices in North Cascades, Cape Flattery, and probably elsewhere, and forages anywhere in lowlands when clouds envelop the mountains. **Vaux's** nests widely in hollow trees, occasionally chimneys.

Behavior: Forage for small insects taken on the wing, anywhere in the sky. Many insects emerge from wetlands, so swifts and swallows fly low over them, especially in bad weather. **Black** tends to fly higher.

Voice: Chip notes. **Black** often in series; **Vaux's** rapid, higher-pitched.

Did you know? Washington's first Black Swift nest was found in 2012 in Whatcom County. Vaux's Swifts roost communally in large numbers in smokestacks and hollow trees in fall migration.

Date & Location Seen: _____

Male

Female

Description: 3.75". MALE: Green back, grayish underparts, **iridescent red crown and throat** (can appear black in shadow), dark tail. FEMALE: Similar except outer tail feathers tipped white, red restricted to small spot on lower throat. IMMATURE: Little or no red.

Similar Species: Female/immature Rufous Hummingbirds (page 259) have rufous sides, undertail, and tail base.

Status and Habitat: Common year-round resident in lowlands, especially cities and towns. Typically in parks and residential neighborhoods, some spillover into countryside. Increasing and spreading. Winter hummingbird feeders and exotic flowering plants, perhaps also climate change, account for phenomenally successful range extension.

Behavior: Consumes nectar from flowers, sugar water from hummingbird feeders, sap from holes in trees (drilled by sapsuckers), small insects, and spiders. Can survive short bouts of severe cold weather by lowering body temperature at night or entering torpor. Males court females with dive displays, ascending 60–120 feet into the air, then zooming down at 385 body lengths/second to pull up with an explosive squeak caused by tail-spreading.

Voice: Loud chip note. Song dry, rasping, delivered year-round from exposed perch. Various squeaks, buzzes, and chattering sounds in courtship and territorial defense.

Did you know? Originally in California north to San Francisco Bay, now breeds north to Vancouver Island, east to Arizona.

Date & Location Seen: _____

_____

Male

Female

Description: 3.25". **Tiny hovering bird** with very slender, straight bill. MALE: **Upperparts and most of underparts rusty-orange;** back may have some green. Crown dull green, **throat iridescent orange-red**, and upper breast white. FEMALE: Upperparts green; **tail base, sides, and undertail rufous**; outer tail feathers white-tipped. Red feathering on throat varies from none to small spot. IMMATURE: Resembles female.

Similar Species: Anna's Hummingbird (page 257) shows no rufous coloration.

Status and Habitat: Common summer resident throughout lowlands and up to tree line in mountains. Males arrive before females in spring, sometimes as early as late February. Occupies forest openings, disturbed areas, and brushy edges. Southbound migrants move up into subalpine meadows in mountains, where many hummingbird-adapted flowers are blooming, in July and August.

Behavior: Consumes nectar from flowers, sugar water from hummingbird feeders, sap from holes in trees, and small insects and spiders. Male has J-shaped dives from well up in air during courtship.

Voice: Chips and other warning notes but no song. Adult male's wings make high-pitched stuttering whine during courtship dive.

Did you know? Rufous Hummingbird is the northernmost representative of this largely tropical New World family. It is also the smallest bird with the biggest attitude in the region.

Date & Location Seen: _____

Male

Female

Description: 12.5". **Large head, bushy crest**, and **long, stout bill.** MALE: Mostly **slaty-blue with white underparts and collar; wide slaty-blue breast band.** FEMALE: Identical but with rufous sides and additional rufous band across lower breast. JUVENILE: Some rufous in upper breast band.

Similar Species: Nothing else in region with the kingfisher's unmistakable voice, behavior, and shape.

Status and Habitat: Common year-round resident. From sea level to tree line, any stretch of shore with good nest sites and fishing prospects has its pair of kingfishers. Such places include rivers, streams, lakes, ponds, and saltwater shorelines with clear, relatively still waters where it can see prey.

Behavior: Watches from perch over water or hovers well above it; plunges to water (penetrating a body length or two below surface) and seizes prey in bill. Takes mostly fish, but a great variety of other animals may enter diet. Digs nest burrows, usually 3–6 feet deep in vertical sand banks.

Voice: Main call loud rattle, somewhat like sound of ratchet noisemaker toy, given all year (often in flight).

Did you know? A Belted Kingfisher returns to its perch with a freshly caught fish in its bill, beats it to death against the perch, then swallows it headfirst.

Date & Location Seen: _____

Description: 10.5". Medium-sized **flycatching woodpecker; iridescent green-black above, glowing pink below**, with dark red face, gray collar and breast. IMMATURE: Face dark, pink barely evident below.

Similar Species: Unique in both color pattern and habits; distant flying bird might be mistaken for small crow.

Status and Habitat: Rare migrant (May, September) in lowlands, more likely in southern part of region. Much more common as breeder and local resident east of Cascades. Breeds in oak woodland and cottonwoods along rivers but migrants may turn up anywhere.

Behavior: Gleans wood-boring insects from trees but does not dig them out like other woodpeckers. Most foraging time spent well above treetops after flying insects, both by sallying like flycatcher or hawking like swallow. Level flight at that time with slow wing-beats presents very different impression from rapid, undulating flights of other woodpeckers. Nuts, especially acorns, prominent in diet, as are fruits of woody plants, including orchard crops.

Voice: Chattering and *churr* calls given mostly by males, probably both aggression and courtship. Many woodpeckers advertise presence by drumming, but this one does so mostly by vocalizations.

Did you know? Lewis's Woodpeckers break up acorns and push pieces of them into crevices to store them for the winter.

Date & Location Seen: _____

Description: 8". Typical woodpecker tree-clinging behavior, undulating flight, and chisel-like bill. Colorful. Breast and **head entirely red** except for faint white mustache mark. Back black with sparse white mottling, belly pale yellow, sides with dusky bars and streaks. Elongated **white patch from wrist out folded wing**, spotted flight feathers. JUVENILE: Dark brownish with sapsucker wing patch, molts to adult plumage by September.

Similar Species: Red-naped Sapsucker (rare in region except at Cascade crest) has white facial lines, no red below throat.

Status and Habitat: Fairly common resident in forests dominated by conifers but also found in various mixed woods. In winter, especially during cold spells, moves into urban parks, backyards, and small woodlots.

Behavior: Quietly drills evenly spaced small holes in live trees, revisiting these "sap wells" on regular foraging routes to drink sap and feed on insects attracted to it. Also takes berries. Moves downslope in winter when sap freezes in favored trees. Excavates nest hole in conifer snag, aspen, or other soft wood.

Voice: Calls include nasal mews and squeals; territorial drumming irregularly spaced (regular in all other woodpeckers).

Did you know? Other animals, including hummingbirds, chickadees, kinglets, and both flying and gray squirrels often feed at sapsucker sap wells.

Date & Location Seen: _____

_____

Downy Woodpecker
Male

Downy Woodpecker
Female

Hairy Woodpecker
Male

Description: 6.25" / 8.5". **Black and white** woodpeckers with **white stripe down back**. Black above, with white head stripes and white-spotted wings; dingy white below. MALE: Red on back of head. JUVENILE: Red crown. **Downy** obviously smaller, with much smaller bill and black spots on outer tail feathers. **Hairy** with bill almost same length as head, unspotted tail feathers.

Similar Species: Red-breasted Sapsucker (page 265) has barred back, white stripe down wing. Three-toed and Black-backed Woodpeckers (page 269) have barred sides, don't show white back stripe.

Status and Habitat: **Downy** common lowland resident in woodlands, parks, residential neighborhoods, stream corridors, and semi-open rural habitats, uncommon at higher elevations. Prefers broadleaf woods but tolerates some conifers. **Hairy** fairly common resident throughout, although scarce in urban areas. Prefers coniferous forest but also uses mixed forest.

Behavior: Both probe limbs and branches in search of insects, **Downy** onto smallest substrates. Excavate nest cavity in dead wood; call and drum to establish territory. Common visitors to suet feeders. Flight undulating as in most woodpeckers.

Voice: Sharp *pik* (louder in **Hairy**) and rattle-like whinny, even in **Hairy** and descending in **Downy**.

Did you know? The two species are rarely seen together because of different habitat preferences.

Date & Location Seen: _____

American
Three-toed
Woodpecker
Male

Black-backed
Woodpecker
Male

Description: 8.5″. Medium-sized woodpecker, black above with **barred back**, white below with **barred sides**. Striped face, white-spotted black wings, and white-edged black tail. MALE: Yellow crown. **Similar Species**: Black-backed Woodpecker (below) with solid black back. Hairy Woodpecker (page 267) with white stripe down back and unmarked sides. Sapsuckers (page 265) with entirely barred back, yellowish underparts. **Status and Habitat**: Uncommon resident of high-elevation conifer forests. **Behavior**: Scales bark off live and dead trees to get at insects beneath. Excavates nest holes in dead trees. **Voice**: Fairly soft *pik* note. **Did you know?** Beetles that lay their eggs in wood come quickly to burned forests, where the dead trees are easy for larvae to bore into. These and other woodpeckers are right behind them, digging out the larvae.

BLACK-BACKED WOODPECKER *Picoides arcticus*

Description: 9″. Medium-sized woodpecker with **solid black upperparts**, striped face, white-spotted black wings, and white-edged black tail. White below with **barred sides**. MALE: Yellow crown. **Similar Species**: See American Three-toed Woodpecker (above). **Status and Habitat:** Uncommon resident of high-elevation spruce/fir/lodgepole pine forests on east side of Cascades, small numbers crossing over to west side. Moves quickly into forests after fires. **Behavior**: Scales bark and excavates to probe for burrowing larvae. Nest holes in dead trees, large clutches of white eggs typical of woodpeckers. **Voice**: Soft *pik*, louder than Three-toed. **Did you know?** Scaled-off bark is a good sign of their presence.

Date & Location Seen: _____

Male

Female

Description: 12″. Robust, colorful woodpecker with long bill, stiff tail, tree-clinging behavior typical of group. Brown above with dark bars, buff below with **black crescent bib** and black spots; **brightly colored feather shafts** most notable in flight. Also shows **white rump** in flight. Two subspecies. Red-shafted with brown cap, gray face, **red shafts**, male with **red mustache mark**. Yellow-shafted with gray cap, brown face, **yellow shafts, red crescent on nape**, male with **black mustache mark**.

Similar Species: No other woodpecker or any other type of bird in region resembles a flicker.

Status and Habitat: Common resident throughout region in open woodlands and urban/suburban areas with scattered trees. Numbers augmented greatly in winter by migrants from the north.

Behavior: Forages on ground for ants and other insects and takes suet and seeds from bird feeders; also seeks fruits in season. Loud calling, drumming (even on houses!), and boisterous interactions make it noticeable in urban areas, where the species increasingly thrives. Excavates cavity nest in live or dead wood, even utility poles. Flight undulating, typical of woodpeckers.

Voice: Calls include *woika woika woika*, long series of repeated *kuk* notes, piercing *keeww*.

Did you know? Red-shafted birds reside year-round in the region. Yellow-shafted birds, migrants from Alaska, are present all winter. Watch for intergrades showing mixed characteristics.

Date & Location Seen: _____

Female

Male

Description: 16". Chisel-like bill, stiff tail, tree-clinging behavior, and undulating flight typical of woodpeckers. **Large and black** except for **crimson crest** and **white neck stripe**, facial markings, underwings, and wing patch. MALE: All red crown and red mustache mark. FEMALE: Forehead and mustache mark black.

Similar Species: Much larger than other woodpeckers in region. Red and white markings and undulating flight distinguish it from crows.

Status and Habitat: Fairly common resident throughout region, including forest tracts and parks within urban areas. Prefers mature coniferous and mixed forests.

Behavior: Excavates large, deep, oval or rectangular holes in trees in search of insects, primarily large beetle larvae and ants. Chisels through hard wood to access insect-damaged tree centers. Also feeds on small fruits. Sometimes loud and obvious with tapping, banging, and calling but also secretive, hiding behind tree trunks. Often calls while flying above or within canopy. Nest hole larger than those of other woodpeckers.

Voice: Series of 10–15 wild-sounding *kuk* notes with irregular rhythm and abrupt ending. Territorial drumming slow and loud.

Did you know? With the extinction of the Ivory-billed Woodpecker of the southeastern United States and Cuba and the Imperial Woodpecker of Mexico, the Pileated Woodpecker is now the largest woodpecker on the North American continent.

Date & Location Seen: _____

Male

Female

Description: 10", wingspan 22"; female larger. **Delicate** small falcon with long, pointed wings, long tail, **russet back**, gray and rufous crown, **two black stripes on white face**. MALE: Blue-gray above, solid russet tail ending in wide black band and narrow white tip. Breast rusty and spotted in adult, streaked in immature. FEMALE: Wings and tail russet with fine barring, breast streaked.

Similar Species: Merlin (page 277) chunkier, darkly streaked below with pale bands on tail, vague mustache mark, more powerful flight. Sharp-shinned Hawk (page 135) with short, rounded wings, faster wing-beat.

Status and Habitat: Uncommon resident in open areas such as farmland, alpine meadows, forest edges, and clearings; numbers augmented by migrants. Sparsely distributed year-round in lowlands. Breeding documented in relatively few areas, more commonly in southern part of region and up in mountains, where present only in summer.

Behavior: Hunts for insects, small mammals, and small birds from perches or by hovering over fields. Nests in natural cavities (usually in trees) but also uses nest boxes. Defends territory by calling and flying at intruders.

Voice: Common call series of piercing *kli* notes.

Did you know? American Kestrels are highly migratory. Winter residents in the Puget Sound Region may be migrants from farther north, while summer residents may go south.

Date & Location Seen: _____

Male

Female

Description: 11", wingspan 22". Compact, **swift-flying** dove-sized falcon. **Heavily streaked below** with plain dark back, **white-banded tail, vague mustache mark**. Appears dark in flight with **sharply pointed wings**. MALE: Adult with gray back and cap. FEMALE: Larger, brown above. JUVENILE: Both sexes brown.

Similar Species: Peregrine Falcon (page 281) larger with prominent mustache mark. American Kestrel (page 275) reddish above, lighter below, and more delicately built, with distinct head markings.

Status and Habitat: Fairly common migrant and winter resident at coastal marshes, agricultural flats, broken woodlands, and urban areas. Rare breeder, mostly in cities with tall trees and good small-bird populations. Easiest to find in cities, towns, or near coastal concentrations of Dunlins.

Behavior: Makes dashing flights from perch and captures prey with blinding speed. Diet almost exclusively small songbirds and shorebirds, except dragonflies important in late summer. Rarely soars but seen in bullet-like passes after prey. Often perches atop prominent snags and conifers. Aggressively harasses other raptors many times its size.

Voice: Rarely vocal away from nest; calls include series of *kee* notes.

Did you know? Nesting in the lowlands of the region, including cities in the northern part, has been increasing over historic levels. Falcons do not make their own nests; this one often uses old crow nests.

Date & Location Seen: _____

Immature

Adult

Description: 22", wingspan 42"; averages, female larger. **Relatively stocky large falcon** with **wing tips short of tail tip** when perched. Plain and finely barred above, white heavily spotted with darker below; **narrow dark mustache stripe.** ADULT: Polymorphic, varying from blackish through gray to mostly white above, heavily spotted below. Skin around eyes and nostrils yellow. IMMATURE: Brown above, heavily streaked below. Skin around eyes and nostrils bluish.

Similar Species: Peregrine Falcon (page 281) slightly smaller, slimmer, longer wings (reach tail tip when perched). Other large raptors with rounded wings.

Status and Habitat: Rare winter resident (October–March) in open habitats. Most often encountered in farmland of lower Samish and Skagit River valleys, could turn up anywhere.

Behavior: Perches on open tree branches, utility poles, and ground. Pursues waterfowl, pheasants, and other birds in powerful flight and strikes them to the ground or water rather than snagging them with talons. Takes more mammals than Peregrine Falcon.

Voice: Silent in winter.

Did you know? Gyrfalcons have always been highly regarded in falconry, usually flown by kings and other rulers. The white ones, unfortunately very rare in the Pacific Northwest, are the *creme de la creme.*

Date & Location Seen: _____

Immature

Adult

Description: 16", wingspan 38"; averages, female larger. Sleek, powerfully built, **crow-sized** falcon with **thick mustache mark,** long **wings reaching tail tip when perched**. Gray above, dark barring below, variable salmon-colored or whitish bib. **Sharply pointed wings** in flight. IMMATURE: Browner with streaking instead of barring; bill and skin around eye pale blue (yellow in adult).

Similar Species: Merlin (page 277) smaller, mustache mark less distinct. Gyrfalcon (page 279) bulkier with shorter, broader wings (wing tips short of tail tip in perched bird). Prairie Falcon (rare in winter) brown, with dark axillars.

Status and Habitat: Uncommon but increasing resident in region, numbers augmented by migrants and wintering birds late September–May. Most common in lowlands; nests in Cascade foothills, San Juan Islands, and cities. Also coastal beaches and tidal flats where migrant shorebirds and waterfowl concentrated. Requires cliffs, tall buildings, and other tall structures for nesting, often near water.

Behavior: Catches live birds in midair, making spectacular dives at speeds up to 200 miles per hour. Prey ranges from songbirds to ducks; Rock Pigeons and shorebirds favored. Nests on bare ledge, fiercely defends territory.

Voice: Calls include harsh, piercing series of *keh* notes.

Did you know? Peregrine Falcons were taken off the Endangered Species List in 1999 after numbers rebounded from pesticide-caused declines.

Date & Location Seen: _____

Olive-sided Flycatcher

Western Wood-Pewee

Description: 7" / 6". Both with **upright stance**, dark grayish olive with hint of crest, long wings (extending farther down relatively shorter tail in **Olive-sided**). **Olive-sided** with wide pale stripe extending from throat down chest to belly giving **vested appearance** (hint of this in **Wood-Pewee**). **Olive-sided** looks larger-headed, with distinctive profile.

Similar Species: **Wood-Pewee** could be mistaken for *Empidonax* species (pages 285–289) but slightly larger, longer-winged, and grayer and lacks an eye-ring (obscure in Willow).

Status and Habitat: Both fairly common May–September residents throughout region. **Olive-sided** prefers fairly mature coniferous forest stands interspersed with open areas, including clearcuts, old burns, and bogs. Declining as breeder in urban areas. **Wood-Pewee** mostly in lowlands but occurs to mountain passes. Prefers open woodlands, woodland edge, and broadleaf growth along watercourses.

Behavior: Both forage from exposed perches, **Olive-sided** right up at treetops, and both make long sallies (**Olive-sided** higher and farther) for flying insects. Both call frequently, best located by voice.

Voice: **Olive-sided** song whistled *quick three beers* with second syllable strongly accented. Calls include *pip pip pip* repeated at short intervals. **Wood-Pewee** call burry, nasal *beezhurr*. Song more extended, given at dawn.

Did you know? Western Wood-Pewees build their nests on the horizontal surfaces of limbs, usually at a fork.

Date & Location Seen:

Description: 5.25". Fairly distinctive member of look-alike *Empidonax* flycatcher group. **Upright stance**; olive-brown above, tan wing-bars, whitish underparts with faint wash of yellow on belly. **Long, broad bill with yellow lower mandible. Eye-ring minimal or absent**. IMMATURE: Buffy wing-bars.

Similar Species: Other *Empidonax* flycatchers in region (pages 287–289) have prominent eye-rings. Western Wood-Pewee (page 283) slightly larger, much darker overall with more crested appearance.

Status and Habitat: Common summer resident (mid May–September). Mostly at lower elevation but also up to mountain passes in appropriate habitat. Nests in open shrubby and wetland habitats, clearcuts, and brushy forest edge, including suburban areas. Nisqually National Wildlife Refuge is a good spot. Scarce in migration away from nesting locations.

Behavior: Forages from perch at edge of small tree or tall shrub, making sallies to capture insects. Eats some berries in summer and fall. Easily located by voice, as distinctive song given throughout day, but especially near dawn.

Voice: Harsh *fitz bew* song, with first syllable strongly accented. Calls include clear *whit*, buzzy *breet*.

Did you know? Identification of *Empidonax* flycatchers is notoriously difficult. Fortunately all of them have distinctive songs, which should be learned, and each species has its own favored habitat.

Date & Location Seen: _____

Description: 5". Difficult to identify member of look-alike *Empidonax* flycatcher group. **Upright stance; appears dark, large-headed**, relatively long-winged. Grayish olive above with white wing-bars, gray head with distinct eye-ring, **dusky gray chest**, yellowish wash on belly. Short bill may appear all dark. IMMATURE: Buffy wing-bars.

Similar Species: Pacific-slope Flycatcher (page 289) slimmer, brighter, with more asymmetrical eye-ring. Willow Flycatcher (page 285) without eye-ring. Both with larger bill, obviously yellow lower mandible. Dusky Flycatcher (rare migrant) paler, with longer bill and tail, different call. Western Wood-Pewee (page 283) larger, no eye-ring.

Status and Habitat: Fairly common summer resident, mid April to September. Nests in older, dense coniferous forests. Scarce on islands and near coast, more common from middle elevations to mountain passes. Widespread in migration, when it can be seen in any forest type.

Behavior: Forages from high perch in conifer, higher than other *Empidonax*; sallies out to capture flying insects. Often flicks tail and wings nervously.

Voice: Song consists of several phrases including burry, distinctive *bureek*. Calls include sharp *peet*.

Did you know? Hammond's Flycatchers can appear brightly colored in fall, as they molt into fresh plumage before migrating. Birds are duller and less yellowish below when worn and faded during summer.

Date & Location Seen: _____

PACIFIC-SLOPE FLYCATCHER
Empidonax difficilis

Description: 5″. Fairly distinctive member of look-alike *Empidonax* flycatcher group. **Upright stance**; olive-green with wing-bars; **yellow wash** on underparts extends up to throat. Wide bill with all yellow lower mandible; strong **teardrop-shaped eye-ring,** pointed behind eye. IMMATURE: Less yellow below, with buffy wing-bars, more difficult to recognize as this species.

Similar Species: Other *Empidonax* flycatchers in region (pages 285–287) less yellow on upper breast and throat, with less prominent, more symmetrical eye-ring. Western Wood-Pewee (page 283) also lacks eye-ring, larger and darker.

Status and Habitat: Common summer resident, mid April to September. Nests throughout region from lowlands to mountain passes, including wooded tracts within urban areas. Prefers shaded interior of moist mixed or coniferous forests, preferably with broadleaf understory. Migrants also use thickets in parks and gardens.

Behavior: Forages by watching for insects while perched within leafy growth, then sallies out to capture prey; stays close to cover. Difficult to see but easily located by distinctive call. May eat some berries, especially in late summer.

Voice: High-pitched, rising, slurred *p-seeet* call; three-part song of thin, squeaky notes heard less frequently.

Did you know? Pacific-slope Flycatcher is distinguishable only by call from the closely related Cordilleran Flycatcher of the interior West.

Date & Location Seen: _____

Western Kingbird

Eastern Kingbird

WESTERN KINGBIRD / EASTERN KINGBIRD
Tyrannus verticalis / Tyrannus tyrannus

Description: 8.5". Both big-headed with **upright stance**, square-tipped, fairly long tail, and broad-based black bill. **Western**: Gray above, paler gray breast, **yellow belly, black tail with white edges. Eastern**: Dark gray above, **white below, black tail with white tip.**

Similar Species: Olive-sided Flycatcher (page 283) smaller with short tail, vested appearance. Tropical Kingbird (rare late fall visitor) similar to Western but tail brown and notched, lacks white edges.

Status and Habitat: Both uncommon to rare, May–August. Common east of Cascades, both have bred in Skagit Valley. Migrants may appear anywhere in open areas. **Western** most likely in May, has nested on South Sound Prairies. **Eastern** has nested at Spencer Island. Both prefer fields and open rural areas with trees for nesting, **Eastern** usually near water.

Behavior: Both forage from prominent perches, including utility wires, flying out to capture insects; **Eastern** also eats fruit. **Western** often nests next to transformers on utility poles so can succeed in treeless landscape.

Voice: Vocal at nest; transients seldom call. **Western** call sharp *kit*. **Eastern** rapid twittering notes.

Did you know? Both species are aggressive toward intruders near their nests, often attacking much larger birds. When displaying, they expose the bright red feathers on the crown that give them their name.

Date & Location Seen: _____

Breeding

Immature

Description: 9.5". Large-headed, long-tailed songbird, mostly pearl-gray, paler below; **face mask, wings and tail black. White marks** in wing and outer tail visible in flight. **Bill large** with slight hook. Immature browner, dark markings less distinct; fine scalloping below (scalloping sometimes also evident in adults).

Similar Species: Loggerhead Shrike (rare migrant) smaller and a bit darker above with wider black mask that crosses over base of its smaller bill.

Status and Habitat: Uncommon winter resident, October to early April. Prefers fields, coastal marshes, and other open places with scattered trees and shrubs in lowlands to lower foothills. Migrants may appear in open areas within cities.

Behavior: Preys on small mammals and birds by hunting from prominent perch, often highest point of shrub, then swooping down and dispatching victim by bite to the neck with hooked bill. Often impales prey on thorn or barbed wire in sheltered location to facilitate feeding or store for later use. Flight slightly undulating with rapid flapping, halting pauses.

Voice: Occasionally offers mellow, warbled phrases of rather beautiful song in winter quarters. Also harsh jay-like call.

Did you know? Northern Shrikes, often called butcherbirds, appear in variable numbers each winter dependent on reproductive success and food supply in the far north.

Date & Location Seen: _____

Description: 5". Compact with short tail, heavy bill. Grayish green above with **gray head, bold well-defined white spectacles**. White below, including throat, with yellowish sides. Prominent **white wing-bars**.

Similar Species: Hutton's Vireo (page 297) smaller and more uniformly colored, diffuse eye-ring broken at top. Other vireos in region lack wing-bars. Red-eyed Vireo (page 299) song sweeter, with complex phrases. Small flycatchers with eye-ring and wing-bars perch upright quietly, then fly out after passing insects.

Status and Habitat: Uncommon summer resident (mid April to September) in coniferous and mixed forests from lowlands up to middle elevations. Migrants widespread anywhere in woodland edge, parks, and neighborhoods.

Behavior: Forages sluggishly and deliberately in upper canopy for insects and small fruits. Inconspicuous unless singing and sings less frequently than other vireos. Joins mixed flocks in migration.

Voice: Song loud, consisting of simple, slurred, burry whistles with pauses between notes tending to be longer than notes themselves. Calls include series of harsh, falling *shep* notes.

Did you know? Closely related and similar in habits and diet, each of the four vireo species of Washington occupies a habitat and usual foraging height at least somewhat distinct from the others.

Date & Location Seen: _____

Description: 4.5". Small, compact, **greenish gray** above, lighter below with **white wing-bars**. Prominent, **diffuse white eye-ring** broken above eye, extending forward to thick, stubby bill. **Feet bluish gray** in all vireos.

Similar Species: Ruby-crowned Kinglet (page 347) common associate in flocks during winter and almost identical, distinguished by smaller size, thin bill, yellowish feet, and black below lower wing-bar. Tends to flick wings more often. Male kinglet's red crown usually hidden. Cassin's Vireo (page 295) larger with longer bill, well-defined spectacled appearance.

Status and Habitat: Fairly common but often overlooked resident in mixed woodlands and thickets from lowlands to moderate elevations in foothills. Typical sites include Discovery Park (Seattle), Watershed Park (Olympia), and Foulweather Bluff Preserve (Kitsap County).

Behavior: Inconspicuous if not vocalizing. Forages deliberately, mostly for insects but takes some berries. Common member of mixed-species foraging flocks outside nesting season. Often found in pairs. Males sing constantly during brief period late winter–early spring.

Voice: Song simple, slurred, whistled *shree* phrase repeated monotonously. Varied calls include rising *bree dee dee* and harsh mewing.

Did you know? Most vireos live in the tropics or migrate there for the winter. Hutton's is the only vireo to remain year-round so far north.

Date & Location Seen: _____

Warbling Vireo

Red-eyed Vireo

WARBLING VIREO
Vireo gilvus

Description: 5". **Plain grayish olive above**, whitish below, with **prominent light eyebrow. Similar Species**: Red-eyed Vireo (below) larger with longer bill, gray cap, eyebrow bordered with black above and below. Other vireos have wing-bars. Warblers yellower, slender-billed. **Status and Habitat**: Common summer resident (May–September) in mixed open woodland and forest edge from sea level to mountain passes; common in urban areas in migration. **Behavior**: Forages for insects mostly in deciduous growth. Joins mixed flocks in migration. Sings often but difficult to spot due to slow foraging style. **Voice**: Song languid, rambling warble, different from other vireos. Calls include nasal mewing. **Did you know?** Vireos weave cup-shaped nests suspended from horizontal forked branches.

RED-EYED VIREO *Vireo olivaceus*

Description: 5.5". Compact, short-tailed. Large, flat-looking head with heavy black bill. **Plain greenish** above and whitish below. **Gray cap, white eyebrow bordered with black line above and below**; red eye. **Similar Species**: Warbling Vireo (above) smaller with shorter bill, lacks black lines bordering eyebrow. Other vireos have wing-bars. **Status and Habitat:** Fairly common summer resident (late May–August) in lowlands, mostly in major river valleys. Prefers mature broadleaf woods, especially cottonwoods along rivers. **Behavior**: Forages leisurely for insects, mostly in canopy. Sings incessantly but difficult to spot. **Voice**: Song continuous, short whistled phrases given every couple of seconds. Calls include mewed *nyeeah*. **Did you know?** Vireos sometimes sing while on their nests.

Date & Location Seen:

Adult

Juvenile

CANADA JAY
Perisoreus canadensis

Description: 10". Distinctive **small-billed gray jay** of coniferous forests. Rather long-tailed and reminiscent of an oversized chickadee. ADULT: dark gray above with fine back streaks, light gray below; **dark cap** set off by white forehead, cheeks, and hindneck. JUVENILE: Dark gray all over.

Similar Species: Other jays (page 303) show much blue. Clark's Nutcracker (page 305) has long bill, short tail, and white in wings and tail.

Status and Habitat: Fairly common in mid- to high-elevation mature coniferous forests. Scattered populations and individuals down to sea level, especially on Olympic Peninsula.

Behavior: Omnivorous, taking everything the forest has to offer, including small animals, bird eggs and young, carrion, berries, even poisonous mushrooms. Curious, begs from tourists, steals food in campgrounds (often called "camp robber"). Breeds very early in spring, stays in family groups until early summer, then dominant juvenile chases others out of territory.

Voice: Contact call often repeated *vik, vik*, also characteristic whistled *whee-ooo*. Some harsher notes. Not as noisy as other corvids but with a wide vocabulary.

Did you know? All corvids (crows and jays) cache food for the winter, but Canada Jays have special salivary glands that allow them to stick their items (up to 1,000 in a day!) to tree branches and needles and lichen clumps.

Date & Location Seen: _____

Steller's Jay

California Scrub-Jay

STELLER'S JAY / CALIFORNIA SCRUB-JAY
Cyanocitta stelleri / Aphelocoma californica

Description: 11″. **Steller's** blue except upper body blackish, with **long, dark crest,** black bars on wings and tail. **Scrub without crest**, blue above with brown back patch, white eyebrow, and dark cheek; **off-white below with white throat and partial blue breast band;** longer tail.

Similar Species: With their blue color and sassy behavior, jays are unique.

Status and Habitat: **Steller's** fairly common resident in coniferous and mixed forests up to tree line, doing well in cities but possibly impacted by nest-raiding crows. **Scrub** uncommon but increasing lowland resident in more open woodland habitats (especially prefers oak woodland) north to Tacoma, increasingly sparse north of that. Both common in urban and suburban areas.

Behavior: Both species omnivorous, eat more seeds in fall and winter, attracted to bird feeders. Secretive when nesting. **Steller's** forages higher in trees but also down to ground. **Scrub** forages more on ground or in brush. Both are gregarious, usually found in pairs and family groups.

Voice: Both species noisy with frequent harsh contact calls, **Steller's** *raak raak raak* and **Scrub** higher-pitched, rising *reeenk*.

Did you know? Jays are among the most intelligent of birds. Both of these species quickly learn to beg for peanuts, which they bury all over their territories and dig up when food is scarce.

Date & Location Seen: _____

Description: 12". Like a **small light gray crow** of the high mountains with **white-marked black wings and tail**. Bill long and slender, wings somewhat pointed.

Similar Species: Mostly gray like a Canada Jay (page 301) and often coming for handouts together with its drab forest-based relative, but the jay has a small bill, short, rounded wings, and a long tail.

Status and Habitat: Common resident of the high Cascades, more local in the Olympics, mostly on the drier northeast side. Occurs where its primary food source, whitebark pine, is common at and just below tree line.

Behavior: Perches up in conifers and conspicuous and noisy flying among them, often well up in the air. Not at all shy about hanging around high-elevation picnic areas to take food from humans.

Voice: Loud and harsh *kraaaa* often calls attention to its presence.

Did you know? Clark's Nutcrackers are among the best-studied caching corvids. A single bird can carry 70 pine seeds in a pouch under its tongue to distances of up to 7 miles and can cache up to 35,000 such seeds in fall and find them again during the winter, even under snow cover! This is a spatial memory to be admired.

Date & Location Seen: _____

_____

Description: 16″. **Completely black** with stout bill and **square (fan-shaped when spread) tail**. Outermost flight feathers narrow, like fingers at ends of wings. JUVENILE: Brownish black with red mouth lining (pale blue eyes when very young).

Similar Species: Common Raven (page 309) larger, with heavier bill, longer wings, wedge-shaped tail, and different voice; soars more, with wings held flat.

Status and Habitat: Common resident in cities, towns, agricultural areas, and river valleys; less common in more remote areas of dense coniferous forest and high mountains. Needs trees for nesting, otherwise ranges widely.

Behavior: Omnivorous, eating anything available. Feeds on refuse, handouts, road kills, crops, fruit, seeds, and insects; raids bird and mammal nests for eggs and young. Intelligent and highly gregarious; forms huge night roosts after nesting season, sometimes numbering in thousands. Harasses predators noisily until they vacate crow territory or remain motionless in cover.

Voice: Noisy, garrulous. Common call *caww*.

Did you know? Crows in our area are currently classified as two species, American Crow and Northwestern Crow. The latter is supposed to be smaller and more coastal. Many ornithologists, however, maintain that there is really only one species since the two forms interbreed freely and are nearly indistinguishable.

Date & Location Seen: _____

Description: 24″. **Largest songbird**, with wingspan almost four feet; same size as Red-tailed Hawk. **Entirely glossy black** with **long, heavy, formidable bill**, long wings, and **long, wedge-shaped tail**. Puffy throat with pointed feathers and head feathers erected in display impart even larger look. Outermost flight feathers narrow at tips, like fingers at ends of wings.

Similar Species: American Crow (page 307) smaller with shorter bill, wings, and tail (not wedge-shaped) and different voice. Ravens soar more often than crows.

Status and Habitat: Fairly common resident throughout region in all habitats away from urban areas. Mostly absent from Everett–Tacoma urban corridor. Perhaps excluded from cities by mobbing crows.

Behavior: Omnivorous, feeding on whatever is available. Specializes in scavenging on large carcasses, often descending on road kills, but also kills rodents, robs nests, and feeds on insects. Highly intelligent and cautious; follows predators and hunters to take advantage of an easy meal. Like all corvids, caches food for future needs. Pairs and groups cavort in aerial displays.

Voice: Varied calls include harsh croak, liquid bell-like sounds, screamed *kraaah*, and metallic rattles.

Did you know? Crows and ravens are always at odds. Ravens raid crow nests. Crows often swoop down on ravens while attempting to chase them away.

Date & Location Seen: _____

Male

Female

Description: 7.25″. Open-country **ground bird** with **reddish brown back and fancy face pattern. Black tail** with white edges conspicuous in flight. MALE: Vivid black markings on head and breast, upper one extended into **tiny feathered horns.** FEMALE: Similar but duller head pattern, no horns.

Similar Species: Sparrows hop, but several other ground birds walk like larks. American Pipit (page 361) has slender bill, no head markings, and finely streaked breast. Lapland Longspur (page 365) has short, conical bill, darker and more heavily streaked above. Snow Bunting (page 365) has short bill and is paler overall, with big white wing patches.

Status and Habitat: One subspecies uncommon summer resident (May–September) on alpine tundra high in Cascades, an arctic-breeding one occasional winter resident (October–March) in coastal areas, a third declining resident in a few areas of prairie, especially Joint Base Lewis-McChord.

Behavior: Forages by walking over open ground seeking insects in summer and seeds in winter. High-elevation birds forage on snow for insects that land there and become cooled; migrate to lowlands after breeding.

Voice: Beautiful tinkling song usually given in flight. Call a musical *su-weet*.

Did you know? The back color of Horned Larks in different populations usually matches the dominant soil color of the region.

Date & Location Seen: _____

Male

Female

Description: 7″. **Large**, long-winged swallow with **shallowly forked tail**, relatively large bill. MALE: Adult **entirely dark purplish blue**. FEMALE: Crown, back, and wings dark purplish blue and brown, **gray-brown of throat and chest extends around neck** in collar; belly dingy whitish. First-year male resembles female with scattered blue feathers below.

Similar Species: Larger than other swallows, soars more. European Starling (page 359) purple-black with similar pointed wings but with long bill and shorter tail. Black Swift (page 255) with much longer, narrower, curving wings.

Status and Habitat: Locally fairly common summer resident (mid April–September) in open areas, mostly near water. In small colonies at scattered coastal locations (Titlow Beach, Budd Inlet); also Ridgefield and Julia Butler Hansen National Wildlife Refuges, Joint Base Lewis-McChord.

Behavior: Forages in flight for insects, often high up. Flocks in migration, sometimes with other swallows. Nests in small colonies, mostly in boxes or gourds provided by humans. Competes with other cavity nesters; sharply declined with European Starling introduction but locally successful in nest sites on pilings over water.

Voice: Song low-pitched, liquid warbles. Calls include rich, descending *chup chew*, rattle in alarm.

Did you know? Eastern Purple Martin populations are highly colonial, using multi-unit nest structures. Western populations are only loosely colonial, shunning martin condominiums.

Date & Location Seen: _____

Tree Swallow

Violet-green Swallow Male

Violet-green Swallow

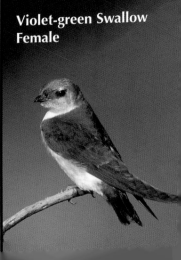

Violet-green Swallow Female

Description: 5.5". Long, pointed wings, notched tail. **Glossy blue above, white below**. FIRST-YEAR FEMALE: Duller, with brown upperparts. **Similar Species**: Violet-green Swallow (below) greener with white flank patches, white extending above eye. **Status and Habitat**: Common summer resident (late February–August) at low to moderate elevation, usually near water. Uses tree cavities or boxes for nest sites. **Behavior**: Forages in flight for insects. Forms large flocks in migration. **Voice**: Song a series of chirps and warbles. Calls include liquid *chweet*. **Did you know?** Providing nest boxes for swallows is mutually beneficial, as they eat mosquitoes and other flies, not to mention the enjoyment of having them around.

VIOLET-GREEN SWALLOW *Tachycineta thalassina*

Description: 5". Long-winged, with notched tail. **White below, extending up sides of rump**. MALE: Glossy, iridescent purple-green above with **white extending above eye**. FEMALE: Bronze-green above, duskier cheek. **Similar Species**: Tree Swallow (above) bluer, with dark around eyes, no flank patches. **Status and Habitat:** Common summer resident (late February–October) from coast to mountains. Woodlands and cities, where declining. **Behavior**: Forages in flight for insects, often at great height. Nests in natural cavities in trees and cliffs, also nest boxes. Large flocks gather before migration. **Voice**: Song repeated *tsip tseet tsip*, reminiscent of Pine Siskin. Calls include *chilip*, higher and sharper than Tree Swallow. **Did you know?** Male Violet-green Swallows sing their courtship song monotonously in the predawn darkness.

Date & Location Seen: _____

_____

Northern Rough-winged Swallow

Bank Swallow

NORTHERN ROUGH-WINGED SWALLOW
Stelgidopteryx serripennis

Description: 5″. **Plain brown swallow** with slightly notched tail. Whitish below, with **dingy gray throat and upper breast. Similar Species:** Female Purple Martin (page 313) larger, more forked tail. Bank Swallow (below) smaller with white throat, brown breast band. Other white-bellied swallows have white throats. **Status and Habitat:** Fairly common summer resident (April–August), mostly at lower elevations. Open areas, usually near water, especially high stream banks. **Behavior:** Forages in flight low over water and fields for insects. Distinctive slow, almost batlike, flight. Uses abandoned burrows of other species and sometimes open pipes for nesting. **Voice:** Call harsh, low *breet*. **Did you know?** "Rough-winged" comes from the small serrations this species shows on its outermost wing feathers.

BANK SWALLOW *Riparia riparia*

Description: 4.75″. Smallest swallow, **brown upperparts and band across breast**; notched tail. **Similar Species:** Brown back, white throat and brown breast band eliminate any other swallows. **Status and Habitat:** Uncommon and local summer resident (May–September) in lowlands, almost always along good-sized rivers such as Skagit, Toutle, and Green that have sand banks for nesting. **Behavior:** Rapid straight flight with fluttery wing-beats over open areas, usually near water. Nests in tight colonies from few birds to hundreds on vertical sand banks, usually over rivers. **Voice:** Call short *bzzht*, almost electronic. **Did you know?** Male Bank Swallows have to follow their mates everywhere to keep other males from attempting to mate with them.

Date & Location Seen:

Description: 5.5". Compact swallow with dark **square tail, rusty-buff rump. Dark chestnut throat and cheeks** contrast with off-white underparts. **Light forehead spot** and buff collar stand out from dark cap and dark back streaked with white. Long, dark, pointed wings, tiny feet and bill.

Similar Species: Other swallows lack very dark throat, orange-buff rump.

Status and Habitat: Common summer resident, April–August; a few linger to September. Widespread in lowlands, ranging up some river drainages into mountains. Prefers open areas, often near water. Large colonies nest on cliffs or human structures such as bridges, dams, and buildings.

Behavior: Forages in flight for insects. Builds gourd-shaped nest on vertical surface with some overhead protection, using mud pellets gathered from wetland edges. Enters nest through short, narrow tunnel. Stages in large numbers away from nest sites when young fledge, then departs for South America, flocking during migration.

Voice: Song thin, harsh twitters, given in series. Calls include husky *churr* and soft, low *veew* given in alarm.

Did you know? Cliff Swallows gathering mud hold their wings up to keep others from trying to mate with them. Pairs defend their nests against other pairs, as females will attempt to lay eggs in nests other than their own.

Date & Location Seen: _____

BARN SWALLOW
Hirundo rustica

Description: 6.75". **Streamlined**, graceful in flight, with long, dark, pointed wings, **long, forked tail** with band of white spots across it. Blue-black above, **cinnamon-buff below** with **dark breast band**, rusty forehead and throat. Tiny bill and tiny feet. IMMATURE: Pale beneath without long outermost tail feathers.

Similar Species: No other swallows are orange-buff below with long, forked tail. Even paler-bellied immatures have distinct forks and white-spotted tails.

Status and Habitat: Common summer resident (mid April–mid September) throughout region; migrants continue through October. Rare but annual in winter. Most common in open habitats with buildings, bridges, and culverts for nesting. Tends to be near water in migration.

Behavior: Forages in flight for insects. Flocks in migration, often with other swallows. Builds nest from mud and grasses lined with feathers, often inside or beneath structures, choosing mostly horizontal ledges but can use vertical surfaces.

Voice: Song string of squeaky, twittering notes and grating sounds. Calls include *kvik*, emphatic *pit veet* given in alarm.

Did you know? The Barn Swallow has adapted nearly completely to nesting on human structures. Nests built in natural sites such as shallow caves and crevices are rarely found. Careful studies have shown that females prefer to mate with longer-tailed males.

Date & Location Seen: _____

BLACK-CAPPED CHICKADEE
Poecile atricapillus

Description: 5″. Typical chickadee, with **white cheek dividing dark cap from black bib**. Short, slender bill. **Cap black, back gray**, belly whitish, sides buffy, wings and tail gray with white edgings. Puget Sound populations smaller and darker than birds east of Cascades.

Similar Species: Chestnut-backed Chickadee (page 327) smaller with sooty-brown cap, chestnut back and sides. Mountain Chickadee (page 325) has white eyebrow and gray sides.

Status and Habitat: Common resident throughout region, absent from higher elevations. Scarce on San Juan Islands, local on Olympic Peninsula. Broadleaf and mixed woods and neighborhoods. Prefers deciduous growth, especially alders.

Behavior: Searches for insects and spiders among branches, hanging upside down to glean leaf undersides. Highly sociable when not nesting, forming small flocks of its own and mixed species. Uses cavities and nest boxes but also excavates own cavity. Common visitor to bird feeders, taking seeds to cache them.

Voice: Song clear whistle. Core Puget Sound populations give 3–6 simple whistles slightly descending, *fee fee fee fee fee*. Populations elsewhere more typical of species, with high *feeee beeee,* with second note lower. Calls diverse but include *chick a dee dee dee*.

Did you know? Chickadees are capable of going into a night torpor, with much-lowered body temperature, saving energy that would have been put into maintaining their daytime temperature of about 100° F.

Date & Location Seen: _____

Description: 5″. Typical black-capped, white-cheeked, black-throated chickadee but with **white eyebrow,** gray sides.

Similar Species: Black-capped Chickadee (page 323) without white eyebrow, has buffy sides. See Black-throated Gray Warbler (page 379).

Status and Habitat: Uncommon resident in coniferous forest high in mountains at eastern edge of region, including Mount Rainier. Usually more open forest than that occupied by Chestnut-backed. Lacking from Olympics. Rarely descends to lowlands in winter, west to the Puget Sound basin, when usually spotted at bird feeders.

Behavior: Typical chickadee, gleaning for insects and their larvae along conifer branches and among needles while in constant motion, in flocks after breeding. Often hangs upside-down to check undersides of branches. Visits seed and suet feeders, sometimes mixed with other chickadee species. Nests in cavities but, unlike Black-capped, does not excavate them.

Voice: Flock call raspy *chick-a-zee-zee-zee*, like Black-capped with sore throat. Spring whistled song *fee-fee-bee-bee*, two pairs of doubled whistles with second pair lower.

Did you know? Mountain Chickadee bill is longer and more slender than that of Black-capped. Careful research with captive birds has shown that this bill is perfectly suited for probing into bundles of conifer needles.

Date & Location Seen: _____

Description: 4.5". Typical chickadee with petite bill, **white cheek dividing dark cap from black bib. Cap and throat sooty-brown; sides and back rich chestnut,** breast and belly off-white. Wings and tail grayish with white edgings.

Similar Species: Black-capped and Mountain Chickadees (pages 323–325) slightly larger with black cap, lack chestnut color. Mountain also with white eyebrow. Dark sides distinctive of Chestnut-backed even in poor light.

Status and Habitat: Common resident throughout region from just below tree line to coast. Breeds in coniferous and mixed forest. Dispersing birds in fall may use deciduous woodlands. Common in urban/suburban settings where conifers present.

Behavior: Forages among branches for insects and spiders, hanging upside down while gleaning from twigs. May form larger flocks than Black-capped but flocks with it and other species. Uses cavities and nest boxes, sometimes in backyards. Visits suet and seed feeders, often caching seeds in tree bark nearby.

Voice: *Zitta zitta zee* call higher-pitched and different cadence than other chickadees in region. Lacks whistled song of Black-capped and Mountain.

Did you know? Historically the most abundant Puget Sound chickadee, the Chestnut-backed is now outnumbered by the Black-capped in many areas where conifers have been replaced by broadleaf vegetation. However, Chestnut-backed still predominates on the Olympic Peninsula and San Juan Islands.

Date & Location Seen: _____

Male

Female

Description: 3.75". **Tiny nondescript long-tailed bird, plain gray-brown** but lighter underneath, browner on head. Bill tiny, black, slightly downcurved. MALE: Eye brown (also in juvenile). FEMALE: Eye white.

Similar Species: Chickadees (pages 323–327) have dark caps and throats, white cheek patches. Kinglets (pages 345–347) have wing-bars and shorter tails.

Status and Habitat: Common resident throughout lowlands, following some river drainages into foothills; numerous in urban areas. Broadleaf and mixed woodlands, open forest, parks, and neighborhoods.

Behavior: Forages in flocks except during short period while nesting. Groups of up to forty individuals move from tree to tree, almost in single file. Feeds mostly on insects, especially scale insects, and spiders; more moth larvae in summer. Often searches beneath branches by hanging tail down; a foraging group looks like a tree of ornaments. Visits suet feeders. Builds extraordinary hanging nest woven of moss, lichens, spider webs, and other materials, up to a foot long with small entrance near top, usually less than ten feet from ground.

Voice: Contact calls given by flocking birds include short *pit*, trilled alarm call.

Did you know? Bushtit nests have an adult pair and usually one or more attendants, typically other males and females that have already lost a nest or are not breeding. Birds circulate freely among nests, nonparents often assisting in parental care.

Date & Location Seen: _____

Red-breasted Nuthatch

White-breasted Nuthatch

RED-BREASTED NUTHATCH
Sitta canadensis

Description: 4.25". **Stubby-tailed**, with straight, chisel-like bill. Gray above, **rusty below**, with **white eyebrow** and **black eye-line**. MALE: Black cap. FEMALE: Gray cap. **Similar Species**: Brown Creeper (page 333) streaked above, woodpeckers much larger. Chickadees have longer tails and white cheek patch. **Status and Habitat**: Common resident from tree line to coast. Numbers increase in lowland areas due to migration and downslope movement in winter. Coniferous and mixed forests and parks, also suburban neighborhoods. **Behavior**: Climbs up and down tree trunks in search of insect prey. Takes seeds in winter, particularly from conifers. Regular at sunflower and suet feeders. Excavates nest cavity in rotten wood. **Voice**: Calls include short nasal *enk* given in series. **Did you know?** Red-breasted Nuthatches smear conifer sap around their nest holes to deter predators.

WHITE-BREASTED NUTHATCH *Sitta carolinensis*

Description: 5". **Long-billed, short-tailed** tree-climbing bird with dark cap, gray back, **white underparts with chestnut undertail.** MALE: Black cap. FEMALE: Gray cap. **Similar Species**: Red-breasted Nuthatch (above) with reddish underparts, white eyebrow. **Status and Habitat:** Uncommon resident of oak woodland from Steilacoom south through Puget Trough. Ridgefield National Wildlife Refuge good spot. **Behavior**: Works tree trunks up, down, and sideways with hitching motions. Long bill effective at digging out insects under bark as well as working on nest cavities. **Voice**: Nasal *ahnk, ahnk, ahnk*, more musical than Red-breasted. **Did you know?** White-breasted Nuthatches in our region are genetically distinct from those to the east and could be a different species.

Date & Location Seen: _____

Description: 5". Slim, **gray-brown above with darker reddish-brown streaks**, plain rusty rump, **white eyebrow**; white below, brightest on chin and breast. **Hitches up tree trunks** with sharp claws and propped on long, stiff tail. Bill long, thin, downcurved.

Similar Species: Red-breasted Nuthatch (page 331) unstreaked, reddish below. Woodpeckers much larger. Bewick's Wren (page 341) sometimes goes up trees; has more uniform brown upperparts and longer, free-wheeling tail.

Status and Habitat: Fairly common resident throughout region, up to mountain passes. Some downslope movement occurs in winter. Mature coniferous forests, open groves, and parks containing good-sized trees; may turn up anywhere in migration.

Behavior: Forages for insects while hitching *up* bark of tree using tail as brace. Probes crevices as it climbs, then flies down onto base of next tree like falling leaf and begins again. Builds nest under sheet of loose bark on trunks and large branches. Joins mixed-species flocks outside nesting season.

Voice: Song high-pitched rising and falling notes in series, often ending on high note. Call high, thin *tseee tseee*, much like Golden-crowned Kinglet calls but almost always two notes.

Did you know? The sight of the Brown Creeper's white breast as it moves up the tree may cause prey to move, facilitating detection.

Date & Location Seen: _____

HOUSE WREN
Troglodytes aedon

Description: 4.5". **Nondescript plain brown, paler below**, with **slender bill**. Fine dark barring on wings and tail, vague line through eye. **Light eye-ring.** Often holds tail at upward angle.

Similar Species: Bewick's Wren (page 341) larger, long-tailed, with bold white eyebrow. Pacific Wren (page 337) darker, with shorter tail. Marsh Wren (page 339) in wet habitat, with whitish eyebrow, streaks on back; plain juvenile more similar to House but buffier.

Status and Habitat: Fairly common but highly local summer resident. Most common in San Juan Islands and Whidbey Island, again from South Sound Prairies south, but rare in many parts of region. Joint Base Lewis-McChord and Fort Casey State Park good bets. Breeds in drier forest edge and semi-open habitats at lower elevations, including clearcuts and suburbs.

Behavior: Forages on ground or fallen logs and in shrubs for insects and spiders. Nests in cavities, including nest boxes. Competes for nest sites with other species, sometimes puncturing their eggs. Males vigorously protect territory with constant singing.

Voice: Song exuberant, bubbling trills given in rapid series. Calls include scolding, rattling, and nasal mewing.

Did you know? House Wrens in one form or another occur from Canada to Tierra del Fuego, among the most familiar birds to people throughout that range.

Date & Location Seen: _____

Description: 3.75". **Tiny**, round-looking **(stubby tail)**, with slender bill and light brown eyebrow. Chocolate brown above, with fine **dark barring on wings, tail, and belly. Breast brown with rufous tinge** and light speckles. Secretive but constantly active.

Similar Species: Bewick's Wren (page 341) larger, with bold white eyebrow. House Wren (page 335) with light breast. Marsh Wren (page 339) with long tail, streaked back.

Status and Habitat: Common resident in dense coniferous and mixed forest with tangled undergrowth and downed logs throughout region from lowlands to mountain passes. Withdraws to below level of heavy snow in winter, when more likely in neighborhoods and parks, but tends to breed away from urbanization. May turn up in yard briefly in migration. Builds mossy nest in crevice in bank.

Behavior: Moves mouse-like through undergrowth, hunting insects and spiders. Investigates intruders from open perch while bobbing up and down. Males sing from perches low and hidden or mid level and exposed.

Voice: Song remarkable lengthy series of varied tinkling trills and warbles; most complex song of any North American bird. Calls include oft-given metallic *chit chit* and rapid staccato series of chips.

Did you know? Pacific Wren has recently been elevated to full species status, distinct from Winter Wren of eastern North America and Eurasian Wren.

Date & Location Seen: _____

Description: 4.5". Secretive but curious marsh dweller. Brown above with **fine dark barring on wings and tail**, plain grayish below; **tail held cocked up**. Dark cap, white eyebrow, and faint **white streaks on upper back**. Long, slender bill. JUVENILE: Back streaks and eyebrow obscure.

Similar Species: House Wren (page 335) plainer with only very faint eyebrow, no back streaks. Bewick's Wren (page 341) larger, with bolder white eyebrow. Pacific Wren (page 337) darker, with short tail.

Status and Habitat: Common resident throughout region at lower elevations, many individuals departing in winter as shallow water freezes. Open freshwater or brackish marshes with thick emergent vegetation, usually cattails. Also salt marshes, river edge, wet fields, even scrub adjacent to wetlands, especially after breeding.

Behavior: Forages low, creeping within thick cover, for insects and spiders. Male sings day or night from exposed or hidden perches with tail cocked, even flat against back.

Voice: Song mechanical but musical rattled trill begun with a few call notes. Males produce individualized songs from over 100 different phrases. Call distinctive, repeated *tik*.

Did you know? Male Marsh Wrens build up to a half-dozen spherical nests amidst emergent stalks; the female chooses one to line and lay eggs in. The number of empty nests may confuse predators.

Date & Location Seen: _____

Description: 5″. Slim, **plain brown** above and whitish below with **bold white eyebrow** and long, slender downcurved bill. Long brown tail with fine dark bands above, black and white bars below. Often flicks tail from side to side.

Similar Species: House Wren (page 335) and Marsh Wren (page 339) with much fainter eyebrows. Pacific Wren (page 337) darker, with stubby tail.

Status and Habitat: Common resident, widespread in lowlands. Primarily an inhabitant of forest edge, hedgerows, thickets, and semiopen habitats, frequent in urban yards.

Behavior: Forages for insects and spiders in dense undergrowth but also probes bark on larger tree limbs and feeds on ground. Nests in natural cavities, often in human-made objects like fence posts or even mailboxes. Very much at home around houses.

Voice: Song extremely variable, loud series of warbles and ringing trills, beginning with soft buzz that sounds like inhalation; easily confused with Song Sparrow. Calls numerous, including harsh scolding notes and sharp *jik*.

Did you know? Bewick's Wren was once more common and widespread in eastern North America than in the West. The situation has reversed in recent decades, eastern populations declining as previously logged forests mature and shrubby areas disappear, while western populations expand as a response to a continued supply of second growth and suburban nest sites.

Date & Location Seen: _____

Description: 7.25". Plump-looking (because of **short tail) uniform slate-gray** riverside bird with slender bill and pale legs. Shape and **bobbing motions** suggest large wren. Often flashes white eyelids. JUVENILE: Slightly paler, with white throat.

Similar Species: Distinctive; much larger than any wren in region and shorter-tailed than other gray songbirds.

Status and Habitat: Uncommon resident on rushing streams and rivers, mostly in mountains from middle elevations up to tree line; may be seen at lower elevation and in more urbanized areas in winter. Moves downstream in winter to larger rivers, even suburban creeks down to their mouths. Check bridge crossings along any river coming out of Cascades or Olympics.

Behavior: Swims like little duck, then dives and "flies" underwater to bottom. Walks along bottom, using wings to stay down and holding on with sharp claws, in pursuit of aquatic insect larvae, mollusks, small fish, and fish eggs. Stands and bobs on streamside rocks, flying up and down stream to feed and protect territory. Builds bulky, domed nests next to streams, often under bridges.

Voice: Song by both sexes a very loud jumble of whistled notes, often repeated, and trills, beginning very early in spring. Calls include buzzy *bzeeet*.

Did you know? Dippers are the only true aquatic songbirds; ours has been known as water ouzel but no relative of European thrushes called "ouzel."

Date & Location Seen: _____

Male

Female

Description: 3.75". **Tiny**, with slender bill, short tail, and constant **nervous wing-flicking**. Olive-gray above, grayish below, with **white wing-bars; flight feathers with golden edging**. Broad white eyebrow below black-striped crown. Crown center orange and yellow in male, yellow in female; colors may be obscured.

Similar Species: Ruby-crowned Kinglet (page 347) with eye-ring, no head stripes. Warblers and flycatchers larger. Yellowish toes and nervous behavior characteristic of kinglets.

Status and Habitat: Common resident throughout region, from tree line in mountains to lowlands. Breeds in conifers, winters there and in mixed woods; migrants appear anywhere, including suburbs.

Behavior: Forages high or low on tiny insects and spiders, although when nesting tends to remain high. Flocks with others when not nesting, also joins rapidly moving mixed flocks. Prefers conifers, especially for nesting, but will forage in any vegetation by gleaning, hanging upside down, and fluttering up to pick prey from underside of branch. Flocks often forage right on ground during adverse weather events in winter.

Voice: Song begins with three high, thin notes, ends with tumbling chatter. Call thin *tsee tsee tsee* or *tsee*, somewhat similar to Chestnut-backed Chickadee, with which it often forages.

Did you know? The English and Latin names of kinglets reflect the jeweled crowns and assertive behavior of these "little kings."

Date & Location Seen: _____

Male

Female

Description: 4". **Tiny, plump-looking, with short tail,** thin bill, and constant, nervous **wing-flicking**. Greenish-gray above, lighter below. Dark wings with white wing-bars, **blackish below lower bar**. Incomplete **white eye-ring**. MALE: Red crown, obscured except when singing and displaying.

Similar Species: Golden-crowned Kinglet (page 345) has light eyebrow below black stripe, no eye-ring. Hutton's Vireo (page 297) very similar but larger with thicker bill, different eye-ring, blue-gray rather than yellowish feet, and lacks black below wing-bar.

Status and Habitat: Common migrant and winter resident in lowlands, September to mid May. Nests in coniferous forest with broadleaf understory high in Cascades and Olympics. Winters throughout lowlands in urban and agricultural settings as well as native woodland. Common up to mountain passes in migration. Prefers thickets, brush, and forest edge in winter.

Behavior: Forages low or high for tiny insects and spiders. Eats some berries, including wax myrtle and poison oak. Congregates in optimal habitats. Prominent member of mixed-species flocks but also forages alone.

Voice: Song surprisingly loud, a long, rolling series of trills, twitters, and repeated phrases, often heard in spring migration. Call low, husky *jidit*.

Did you know? Curious and easily attracted, male Ruby-crowned Kinglets display their red crowns aggressively when agitated.

Date & Location Seen: _____

Western Bluebird
Male

Western Bluebird
Female

Mountain Bluebird
Male

Mountain Bluebird
Female

Description: 6.5″. Small **upright thrush**. MALE: Bright blue above with **rusty-brown breast and sides,** pale gray belly. FEMALE: Less blue, paler overall. JUVENILE: Back and breast pale-spotted. **Similar Species**: Mountain Bluebird (below) lacks rusty tones on breast. Male Lazuli Bunting (page 409) smaller with white wing-bars, finch-like bill. **Status and Habitat**: Uncommon summer resident (March–August) in open woods, clearcuts, and farmlands in lowlands. Rare in winter. Good populations in South Sound Prairies. **Behavior**: Forages on insects, also berries in fall. Hunts from low perch, often hovering. Both bluebirds flock outside nesting season and are cavity nesters, readily accepting nest boxes. **Voice**: Seldom sings. Calls include low whistled *chwer*. **Did you know?** Bluebirds returned to the Joint Base Lewis-McChord prairies thanks to provision of nest boxes.

MOUNTAIN BLUEBIRD *Sialia currucoides*

Description: 6.5″. Small **upright thrush** of open country. MALE: Entirely sky-blue, paler below. FEMALE: brown with bluish wings and tail. JUVENILE: Like female but underparts obscurely streaked with brown. **Similar Species**: Western Bluebird (above) with rusty breast. **Status and Habitat**: Uncommon summer resident in subalpine meadows in Cascades; rare migrant and winter resident in open lowland areas. **Behavior**: Perches on outer tree branches, tops of shrubs, and fences and wires. Flies out to capture insects on ground. Often hovers while foraging. **Voice**: Robin-like morning song and soft, repetitious warble; all-year call nasal *tew*. **Did you know?** Very different from most thrushes, it has been called a "scaled-down version of an American Kestrel."

Date & Location Seen: _____

Description: 8″. Short-billed, **long-tailed, all gray** thrush with prominent **white eye-ring** and **buffy wing patches**.

Similar Species: No other mostly gray long-tailed songbird except very differently patterned shrikes (page 293); rare Northern Mockingbird, larger and longer-billed with white wing patches and no eye-ring; and even rarer Gray Catbird (breeds east of Cascades), dark gray with black cap and rusty undertail coverts.

Status and Habitat: Fairly common summer resident (May–September) in mountain coniferous forests, uncommon spring and fall migrant from alpine zone to coast, and rare winter resident in lowlands. Can be anywhere wooded but often found at juniper trees in winter.

Behavior: Perches conspicuously in open from low branches to treetops. Flycatches from elevated perch during summer, taking flying insects in lengthy flights or, more commonly, pouncing on ground dwellers from low perch. Switches to largely fruit diet in fall and winter. Eats a wide variety of fruits, including currants, mountain ashes, and cherries, but prefers juniper berries, available through winter.

Voice: Loud robin-like song given from treetops throughout year; bell-like *tew* calls also used for territoriality.

Did you know? Because of their low moisture content, juniper berries are a more concentrated source of energy than fruits of broadleaf trees and shrubs. A solitaire may feed entirely on them and consume 50,000 during a winter.

Date & Location Seen: _____

Swainson's Thrush

Hermit Thrush

Description: 6.75". **Plain warm brown above** from head to tail. Buff breast with small dark spots. Face with diffuse **buffy eye-ring** extending to bill, giving **spectacled appearance**. **Similar Species**: Hermit Thrush (below) with contrasting rusty tail, white eye-ring, habit of cocking tail. **Status and Habitat**: Common summer resident (mid May–early September) throughout region up to mountain passes. Mostly breeds away from urbanized areas. Migrants secretive but widespread. Leafy deciduous or mixed forest with dense understory of salmonberry and other shrubs. **Behavior**: Forages on ground and in trees on insects and berries. **Voice**: Song a series of ethereal nasal whistles spiraling upward. Calls include low, whistled *whit*. **Did you know?** Our Swainson's Thrushes winter in western Mexico and northern Central America.

HERMIT THRUSH *Catharus guttatus*

Description: 6". **Plain brown upperparts contrast with reddish brown tail**. Buffy-white breast with dark spots, gray flanks. **Narrow white eye-ring. Similar Species**: Swainson's Thrush (above) has brown tail, rarely cocks it. Fox Sparrow (page 391) with conical bill. **Status and Habitat:** Fairly common breeder in coniferous and mixed forests, including regenerating clearcuts, at high elevations. Common but secretive migrant and uncommon winter resident in lowland thickets and forest edge. **Behavior**: Forages on or near ground for insects and fruit. Often cocks tail, then slowly lowers it. **Voice**: Song starts with pure whistle, then ethereal, spiraling whistles at different pitches. Calls include muffled *chup*. **Did you know?** Hermit Thrushes sometimes stir leaf litter with one foot to flush prey.

Date & Location Seen: _____

Male

Female

Juvenile

Description: 9.5″. Familiar bird with fairly long tail, **dull orange underparts**. Slender **yellow bill, white marks above and below eye,** dark streaks on white throat, and white undertail. MALE: Darker, head blackish. FEMALE: Breast lighter orange, head paler. JUVENILE: Spotted breast and back.

Similar Species: Varied Thrush (page 357) with head stripes and breast band. Other thrushes smaller, without orange breast. Spotted Towhee (page 385) smaller, with white belly.

Status and Habitat: Ubiquitous common resident in region, coast to mountains. Forests, parks, and suburbs with lawns and other open areas for foraging. Nests wherever trees or other structures present for nest placement and mud available for nest lining.

Behavior: Runs on ground or stands still while searching for insects and earthworms. Takes fruits from shrubs, trees, and ground. Winter flocks can number in hundreds. Roosts communally at night in dense vegetation, often near fruiting trees. May migrate if driven south by cold but usually returns north as soon as temperature allows.

Voice: Song familiar lengthy, rich caroling, consisting of rising and falling phrases. Calls include *tuk tuk tuk*, sharp *piik* given in alarm, and high, thin *sree-reep* in flight.

Did you know? Wandering flocks of robins sometimes descend on fruiting trees and shrubs and strip them clean of berries in a matter of hours.

Date & Location Seen: _____

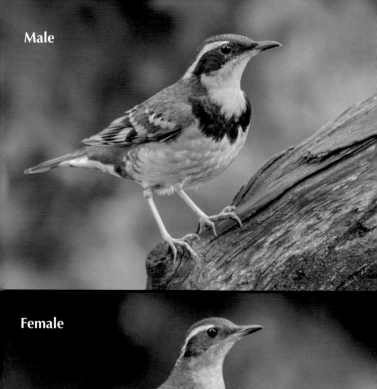

Male

Female

Description: 9″. **Large thrush with short tail, dark mask and breast band. Orange eyebrow,** throat, breast, and wing markings. MALE: All **bluish gray** above, breast band and mask black. FEMALE: Brownish-gray mask and upperparts, with **faint breast band.**

Similar Species: American Robin (page 355) with longer tail, no head pattern or breast band.

Status and Habitat: Common resident. Breeds in moist coniferous forest with thick understory, winters in greater variety of wooded habitats including suburbs. Now breeds primarily in mountains due to fragmentation of lowland forests. Fairly common in lowlands by October, leaves in April. Vacates areas as snow depth increases.

Behavior: Forages for fruits in trees and shrubs and insects and other invertebrates on ground. Exposes prey by poking bill in leaf litter and throwing leaves around. Eats much fruit in winter but also hangs out under suet feeders for pieces knocked loose by woodpeckers. Rarely in loose flocks, often flushing from roadside in wooded areas.

Voice: Song heard all year long, a fairly long, ethereal, trilled whistle, repeated at different pitches after long pauses. Calls include *chup* similar to Hermit Thrush.

Did you know? If birds were newly named based on their attributes, this one might be called Ruddy-breasted Leaftosser. Bits of the substrate fly in all directions when a thrush is on the hunt.

Date & Location Seen: _____

Breeding

Nonbreeding

Juvenile

Description: 8″. Blackbird-looking with **short tail** and **long, pointed bill.** Pointed wings and short tail impart **triangular appearance** in flight. BREEDING: Looks black but in good light **iridescent purple and green** with minimal brown feather edging and **yellow bill.** Male bill pale blue at base, female pale pink. NONBREEDING: Heavy pale spotting and wide brown feather edging throughout; dark bill. JUVENILE: **Plain grayish brown.**

Similar Species: Western Meadowlark (page 413) with white outer tail feathers, yellow breast. Blackbirds with longer tails, more conical bills.

Status and Habitat: Common resident throughout region in altered habitats such as cities, suburbs, parks, open woodland, and farms. Scarce in mountains and forest. Original range Eurasia; introduced in many other parts of world, including North America.

Behavior: Probes ground for insects. Forages in trees or on ground for whatever available, often flycatches like swallows when insects swarm. Feeds in flocks, gathers by thousands at evening roosts. Competes for nest cavities with native species and may displace them. Sings year-round from prominent perches, sometimes while flapping wings like wind-up toy.

Voice: Continuous series of squeaks, squawks, and whistles, including mimicry of other species.

Did you know? Starlings don't molt into breeding plumage. Instead, the pale tips of the feathers grown in fall wear off continuously through the winter, culminating in that glossy plumage in spring.

Date & Location Seen: _____

_____

Breeding

Nonbreeding

Description: 6″. Sparrow-like but with long, slender bill and fairly long **white-edged tail**. Plain gray-brown above with faint wing-bars and feather edging. Underparts light buff to white, variably **streaked** on breast. Light eyebrow and eye-ring. **Wags tail up and down while walking.**

Similar Species: Thin bill and tail-bobbing habit separate pipits from sparrows and longspurs (Vesper Sparrow and Lapland Longspur have white-edged tails). See Palm Warbler (page 367), somewhat similar tail-bobber.

Status and Habitat: Local but fairly common breeder on alpine tundra in high Cascades and Olympics, regular at Mount Baker, Mount Rainier, and Hurricane Ridge. Widespread and fairly common spring and fall migrant, although uncommon in urban areas, and uncommon in winter in lowlands. Typically at plowed fields, meadows, dried pond margins, and beaches.

Behavior: Usually walks on ground, foraging primarily for insects, also seeds in migration and winter. Flocks at all seasons except when nesting. Can be tame and approachable, but entire flock may flush if alarm call given. Birds fly in loose flocks, each bird descending to ground in characteristic stair-step fashion.

Voice: Sharp distinctive *tsi tsip* call, given often in flight.

Did you know? American Pipits in breeding plumage are somewhat more lightly streaked and buffier beneath than in nonbreeding plumage. Some breeding individuals may be completely unstreaked.

Date & Location Seen: _____

_____

Bohemian Waxwing

Cedar Waxwing

Description: 7.5" / 6.5". Both species **sleek and crested** with silky-brown head and back grading into gray rump and brown underparts. **Black mask and chin**, plain gray wings with **waxy red feather tips**. Short dark tail with **yellow tip. Bohemian** with **white and yellow patches** in wings, **chestnut undertail. Cedar** with **yellowish belly, white undertail**. JUVENILE: Duller with streaks below, no waxy tips.

Similar Species: Distinctive. European Starling (page 359) has same pointed-winged shape in flight, especially like similar-sized Bohemian, but darker and shorter-tailed, with different markings.

Status and Habitat: Cedar common summer resident throughout region, most moving south by November, returning in mid May. Largest flocks appear in fall, include many juveniles. **Bohemian** scarce and erratic winter visitor, more common in northern part of region. Both species in open forest, forest edge, city parks, and suburbs near ornamental plantings.

Behavior: Both eat mostly small fruits, including Pacific madrone and mountain ash. **Cedar** takes insects and often flycatches during summer. Both flock after nesting, descending on ripe fruit trees en masse. Tight, swirling flocks can number in hundreds. Both call frequently in flight and while perched.

Voice: Call high-pitched, thin *sreeee*, louder in **Bohemian**.

Did you know? Cedar Waxwings nest late to exploit the availability of ripe fruit. Bohemian Waxwings aren't present in western Washington every winter.

Date & Location Seen: _____

Lapland Longspur
Nonbreeding

Snow Bunting
Nonbreeding

Description: 6". **Sparrowlike ground feeder** with **bright head pattern.** BREEDING MALE: **Black crown and throat** bordered by white and then **rufous nape.** Back brown and streaky, sparrowlike. BREEDING FEMALE: Streaked cap, dark cheek patch, pale throat. NONBREEDING: Sparrowlike above, mostly white below with **dark-bordered cheek patch. Similar Species**: Cheek patch allows distinction from all sparrows. **Status and Habitat**: Uncommon spring (April–May) and fall (September–October) migrant in lowlands, especially along coast. Rarely winters. Open fields and beaches. **Behavior**: Forages for seeds on ground by walking. May be in loose flocks in migration. **Voice**: Musical *tew* note and staccato rattle in flight. **Did you know?** Like starlings, Lapland Longspurs change into bright spring plumage by wear rather than molt.

Description: 6.5". MALE: **Sparrowlike ground feeder** with big **white wing patches.** BREEDING MALE: **Black back**, outer wing feathers and tail; **white head**, underparts, and outer tail feathers. BREEDING FEMALE: Streaks on head and back instead of solid black. White wing patch smaller. NONBREEDING: **Russet-brown head and breast markings**, streaked back, and white underparts. **Similar Species**: Unique white wing patches evident on perched bird, dramatic in flight. **Status and Habitat:** Uncommon winter visitor (October–February) in lowlands, mostly near coast. **Behavior**: Individuals or small flocks forage for seeds on ground in open country. **Voice**: Call melodious, rolling *tirr-rrip*. **Did you know?** Snow Buntings are very early migrants, so they leave the Pacific Northwest while still in nonbreeding plumage.

Date & Location Seen: _____

American
Redstart
Male

American
Redstart
Female

Palm Warbler

AMERICAN REDSTART
Setophaga ruticilla

Description: 4.75". Active warbler that fans long, colorful tail. MALE: **Black head, breast, and upperparts**, white belly. **Orange patches** on sides of breast, wings and much of tail base. FEMALE: Olive-gray above, whitish below, with **yellow patches**. **Similar Species:** No other small songbird similarly colored. **Status and Habitat:** Uncommon and very local summer resident (late May–September) in riparian woodland up against Cascades foothills. Upper Skagit River Valley best area. **Behavior:** Active forager, moving rapidly with tail fanned and wings drooping to show color patches. Many insects caught by flycatching. **Voice:** Song a series of thin, sibilant notes. Call a liquid chip. **Did you know?** First-year males look like females but sing and attempt to breed.

PALM WARBLER *Setophaga palmarum*

Description: 4.75". Dull **ground-foraging, tail-wagging** warbler. Brown above with strong whitish eyebrow, whitish below with blurry breast streaks; **yellow under tail.** Spring birds with rufous cap and yellow throat. **Similar Species:** Yellow undertail, pale eyebrow, and lack of wing-bars distinguish from Yellow-rumped Warbler (page 377), more obscure breast streaks and smaller size from American Pipit (page 361). **Status and Habitat:** Uncommon winter resident (October–February), rarely staying into spring. Prefers open areas with scattered to fairly dense shrubs. Westward movement concentrates birds at coast. **Behavior:** Forages for insects mostly on ground, usually wagging tail up and down continuously. **Voice:** Light chip note. **Did you know?** Ground-feeding birds may wag their tails to startle potential insect prey into moving.

Date & Location Seen: _____

Orange-crowned Warbler

Nashville Warbler

ORANGE-CROWNED WARBLER
Oreothlypis celata

Description: 4.5". **Plain yellowish green** with vague breast streaks. Best mark **faint dark line through eye** and light line above it; male's dull orange crown sometimes visible. Breeding birds **quite yellow below.** Migratory northern subspecies duller, gray-headed. **Similar Species**: Yellow Warbler (page 375) plain-faced with larger bill. Female Wilson's Warbler (page 383) shows vague dark cap, often elevates tail. **Status and Habitat**: Common summer resident (April–October) throughout region to tree line; rarely in winter. Breeds in brushy forest edge, including regenerating clearcuts. Migrants anywhere, including overgrown blackberry thickets and hedgerows. **Behavior**: Forages relatively low on insects, also takes fruit and visits suet feeders. **Voice**: Song colorless trill that drops off at end. Call high, sharp chip. **Did you know?** Orange-crowned Warblers feed at sapsucker wells in winter.

NASHVILLE WARBLER *Oreothlypis ruficapilla*

Description: 4.5". Olive above, **yellow below,** whitish on lower belly; **gray head** and **white eye-ring**. Hidden rufous crown patch shown by displaying males. **Similar Species**: MacGillivray's Warbler (page 371) has gray throat and breast. **Status and Habitat:** Uncommon and local summer resident (May–August) here and there in Cascades foothills and migrant through lowlands. Breeders prefer forest edge with abundant deciduous shrubs and small trees, migrants anywhere. **Behavior**: Forages by gleaning vegetation for insects and spiders, mostly middle to low levels. **Voice**: Song a rapid series of single or double chips. Call sharp chip. **Did you know?** Because of their use of second growth, Nashville Warbler populations are faring well.

Date & Location Seen: _____

Male

Female

Description: 5″. Skulking warbler, **olive above** with **plain wings, gray hood, white crescents above and below eye, yellow lower breast and belly.** MALE: Hood bluish gray; blackish markings through eye and on breast. FEMALE: Duller with less distinct eye crescents, no black markings.

Similar Species: Gray-headed form of Orange-crowned Warbler (page 369) similar but much duller, faint eye crescents. Nashville Warbler (page 369) lacks hood, has yellow throat and complete white eye-ring.

Status and Habitat: Fairly common summer resident (mid April–early September) from lowlands to near tree line. Breeders avoid urban areas. Migrants secretive, seldom seen. Forest edge with dense understory, including recent clearcuts, burns, and early second growth.

Behavior: Quite difficult to see as it forages for insects and spiders under cover in dense, low growth. Male sometimes sings from exposed elevated perch. Pairs greet intruders with loud call notes.

Voice: Song rhythmic series of short, buzzy phrases with last notes lower-pitched, slurred. Calls include loud, sharp *tsik*.

Did you know? MacGillivray's Warbler was first described by the American naturalist John Townsend, who discovered it near Vancouver, Washington, and named it after American ornithologist W. T. Tolmie in 1839. John James Audubon at almost the same time named it for Scottish naturalist William MacGillivray. Thus the discord between common and scientific names.

Date & Location Seen: _____

Male

Female

Description: 4.75". Wren-like warbler, olive-brown above and on sides with **yellow throat, breast, and undertail**. Wings unmarked, sides brownish, and belly grayish white. MALE: **Black "bandit" mask** bordered by white above. IMMATURE MALE: Much reduced mask. FEMALE: Without mask, browner.

Similar Species: Other yellowish warblers lack mask, brownish sides, and whitish-gray belly, unlikely in wetland habitat.

Status and Habitat: Common summer resident throughout lowlands, April–September; rarely lingers into winter. Breeds in low, dense wetland vegetation (cattails, shrubs, and boggy areas) but also uses brushy, early-succession fields. Nisqually and Ridgefield National Wildlife Refuges, Montlake Fill, and Skagit Wildlife Area typical sites. Rare in migration away from nesting habitat.

Behavior: Creeps through thick cover foraging for insects and spiders, as well as small amount of seeds. Sometimes feeds on ground. Male sings persistently, body upright, from elevated perches. In courtship, male may perform flight display in which it rises up to 100 feet in the air, giving complex and lengthy song.

Voice: Song whistled *witchety witchety witchety witchety*. Calls include oft-given *chep*, electric *bizz*.

Did you know? Described by Linnaeus in 1766 from Maryland, the Common Yellowthroat was one of the first birds to be described from the New World.

Date & Location Seen: _____

Male

Female

Description: 4.5". **Yellow head and underparts**, darker olive-yellow above; wings with lighter feather edges and yellow spots in relatively short tail. **Dark eye prominent on plain face.** MALE: Bright yellow with distinct **reddish brown breast streaks.** FEMALE: Duller, no breast streaks; can show **indistinct yellow eye-ring.**

Similar Species: Wilson's Warbler (page 383) female with longer tail held up, indication of dark cap. Orange-crowned Warbler (page 369) duller, with faint line through eye. Common Yellowthroat (page 373) female with brownish sides, grayish belly.

Status and Habitat: Common summer resident throughout region, May–September. Spring migrants continue to pass through into early June; fall movement begins in late July. A riparian bird, breeding near water at woodland edge and in shrubby areas with cottonwoods and willows. Migrants more widespread but not often seen in urban areas.

Behavior: Forages for insects and spiders by gleaning at various heights. Males feed higher in canopy than females. Joins mixed flocks in migration.

Voice: Song *sweet sweet sweet I'm so sweet*. Call notes include thin *tsip* and loud chip.

Did you know? Brown-headed Cowbirds often lay eggs in Yellow Warbler nests. To foil them, the warblers sometimes build a new nest over the top of all the eggs and lay a fresh set.

Date & Location Seen: _____

_____

Audubon's
Breeding Male

Myrtle
Breeding Male

Audubon's
Nonbreeding

Description: 5.25". **Yellow rump** and sides of breast; **white tail spots**. Male in breeding plumage has small yellow crown patch (sometimes obscured), black-streaked gray back, **black breast with sides streaked down to white belly. Brown in winter with streaked breast.** Two easily recognizable subspecies. Myrtle with **white throat, black mask**, white wing-bars. Audubon's with **yellow throat**, gray head, **solid white wing patch.** Females of both duller than males and with streaked breast. In winter, Audubon's head plainer than Myrtle and yellowish throat evident.

Similar Species: Distinctive in breeding plumage. In winter, separable from sparrows by thin bill, yellow rump, and foraging behavior.

Status and Habitat: Audubon's common summer resident in fairly open coniferous forest, more so in mountains; abundant in migration and winters in small numbers throughout. Myrtle common in migration, small numbers winter primarily along coast. Both winter in agricultural areas, brushy woods, and coastal scrub.

Behavior: Forages for insects and spiders among leaves and twigs; also frequently flycatches. Travels in loose flocks outside breeding season, when fruit intake increases (wax myrtle gives Myrtle its name); also visits suet feeders.

Voice: Variable, two-part song a clear, warbled trill, usually rising or falling at end. Myrtle call loud *tup*, Audubon's weaker *chit*.

Did you know? The two subspecies were long considered separate species.

Date & Location Seen: _____

Male

Female

Description: 4.75". **Black and white head pattern** with **small yellow spot in front of eye**; gray back, white wing-bars, **white below with dark side streaks**; white outer tail feathers. MALE: Black cap, cheek, and extensive bib. FEMALE: Crown and cheek grayer, throat white with bib reduced (can be absent in immature).

Similar Species: Townsend's Warbler with yellow underparts, Hermit with yellow head (both page 381). Chickadees (pages 323–327) with entirely white cheeks, no streaks.

Status and Habitat: Fairly common summer resident (mid April–September) throughout lowlands; a few linger later. Breeds in mature deciduous and mixed forest but seldom nests in urbanized areas. Migrants widespread and in more varied habitats. Good sites include Nisqually National Wildlife Refuge, middle reaches of Snoqualmie River, and Skokomish River Valley.

Behavior: Forages for insects and spiders at various heights in canopy. Gleans, hovers, and sallies for prey. Joins mixed-species flocks in migration.

Voice: Song variable, husky series of buzzy notes with emphatic ending. Calls include low, dull *tup*.

Did you know? In much of their breeding range to the south, Black-throated Gray Warblers are associated with oak forests, quite different from their haunts of alder and maple woods with scattered conifers in the Pacific Northwest.

Date & Location Seen: _____

Townsend's Warbler
Male

Hermit Warbler
Male

Description: 4.75". MALES of both with gray to greenish back, **black throat**, white belly, prominent **white wing-bars**, and white outer tail feathers. **Townsend's** with **black and yellow head pattern, yellow breast with dark streaks** at sides. **Hermit** with **all yellow head, white unstreaked breast**. FEMALES similar but throat pale. IMMATURES: **Townsend's** with head pattern more obscure.

Similar Species: Black-throated Gray Warbler (page 379) lacks yellow except for spot in front of eye. Yellow-rumped Warbler (page 377) with subterminal white spots in tail, good distinction in overhead flight high in conifers.

Status and Habitat: **Townsend's** common summer resident in mature coniferous forest, mostly well up in mountains (Mount Rainier, higher Olympics). **Hermit** in similar habitat but from about Mount Adams and east side of Olympics south (Capitol State Forest good). **Townsend's** uncommon in lowlands in winter, **Hermit** absent.

Behavior: Both glean and hover-glean for insects and spiders high in canopy. **Townsend's** joins mixed-species flocks in winter and visits suet feeders.

Voice: Both have buzzy song, variable with several evenly pitched notes followed by thin, high notes. **Hermit** song softer and clearer. Call quiet but sharp chip.

Did you know? These two warblers often hybridize, resulting in intermediate offspring. Dominance of Townsend's genes in hybrid zones has resulted in Hermit's range retreating southward.

Date & Location Seen: _____

Male

Female

Description: 4.5". **Olive-green above, yellow below,** brightest on plain face; **wings plain.** Long tail flicked sideways, also cocked above back and waved frequently. MALE: **Round inky-black cap.** FEMALE: **Indistinct cap** makes yellow eyebrow stand out; some females with black cap like males. IMMATURE: Cap blends with back.

Similar Species: Yellow Warbler (page 375) female with shorter tail, lacks any trace of cap. Female Common Yellowthroat (page 373) much duller, with brownish sides. Nashville Warbler (page 369) with mostly gray head. Orange-crowned Warbler (page 369) with faint eye-line, much duller yellow.

Status and Habitat: Common summer resident (mid April–mid September) throughout region up to tree line, but nesting uncommon in urban areas. Common migrant in all habitats. Extremely rare in winter. Nests in moist tangles and thickets near openings in deciduous or mixed woods, including regenerating clearcuts.

Behavior: Flits through foliage, mostly in understory. Sallies for and gleans small insects and spiders from small branches and leaves. Sings constantly in spring.

Voice: Song emphatic series of slurred chips that builds in volume and speed. Call soft, nasal *timp*, quite different from other warblers.

Did you know? Wilson's Warbler and four other American bird species are named for pioneering Scottish-American ornithologist Alexander Wilson.

Date & Location Seen: _____

Male

Juvenile

Female

Description: 7.5". **Dark hood** and upperparts contrast with **rufous sides** and **white belly. Bold white spots on back and white corners on long tail.** Dark conical bill, red eye. Male black, female very dark gray-brown. JUVENILE: Heavily streaked, lacks hood.

Similar Species: Dark-eyed Junco (page 403) smaller, bill pinkish, entire tail edge broadly white, and lacks white back spots. Smaller size and lack of white tail corners separate streaked sparrows from juvenile towhee.

Status and Habitat: Common resident throughout region except withdraws from higher elevations in winter. Open woods with dense shrubby understory, thickets, and overgrown fields. Absent from closed-canopy forests. Thrives in urban areas, nesting in backyards.

Behavior: Forages mostly on ground for seeds, insects, and fruits. Jumps up and scratches ground vigorously with both feet at once while feeding. Does not flock, although found with other sparrows. Readily comes to feeders with all kinds of seeds.

Voice: Song a variable, buzzy trill, similar in adjacent males but varying greatly in populations. Call given often, a rising *shreeee* not so different from a cat's meow.

Did you know? The "double-scratch" of a towhee is noisy enough to be a good sign of its presence, although Fox Sparrows and sometimes Song Sparrows do the same.

Date & Location Seen: _____

American Tree Sparrow

Chipping Sparrow

Description: 5.75". Slender-looking small sparrow. **Rufous cap and eye-line** on gray head. Back gray and brown striped, prominent white wing-bars. Underparts gray with brownish tinge and **black spot on center of breast. Similar Species**: Chipping Sparrow (below) smaller, with white eyebrow. No other plain-breasted sparrow has black breast spot. **Status and Habitat**: Quite uncommon winter visitor (October–March), usually at edge between open ground and small trees. **Behavior**: Forages for seeds and insects on ground, retreats to shrubs and trees when disturbed. **Voice**: Call musical *tee-chup* in flocks. **Did you know?** The best way to find rare sparrows is to check mixed feeding flocks.

CHIPPING SPARROW *Spizella passerina*

Description: 5". **Small** long-tailed sparrow with streaked back, **unmarked gray breast. BREEDING: Rufous cap bordered by white eyebrow,** black line through eye. NONBREEDING: Browner; cap dull and streaked. **Similar Species**: American Tree Sparrow (above) similar but with breast spot, rufous eye-line. Other small sparrows shorter-tailed. **Status and Habitat:** Fairly common but very local summer resident in region. Mostly drier places, including South Sound Prairies and San Juan Islands; also near mountain passes. Open woods and woodland edge with grassy areas. **Behavior**: Forages mostly on ground for seeds and insects. Seldom observed in flocks. **Voice**: Song mechanical-sounding long trill, all on one pitch. Calls include sharp chip, thin *seet*. **Did you know?** Chipping Sparrows make use of animal hair in building their nests. Woven hair makes up the bulk of the nest in some cases.

Date & Location Seen: _____

_____

Vesper Sparrow

Savannah Sparrow

Description: 6″. Medium-sized sparrow, **heavily streaked above and on breast** with whitish belly. **White eye-ring and outer tail feathers.** Lesser coverts ("wrist") rufous, not always exposed. **Similar Species**: Savannah Sparrow (below) lacks conspicuous eye-ring and white outer tail feathers. All other sparrows darker. Lapland Longspur (page 365) has different cheek pattern. **Status and Habitat**: Uncommon and local summer resident in lowlands, breeding in grasslands as at Mima Mounds. Migrants from interior can turn up anywhere. **Behavior**: Forages on ground for seeds and insects. Males sing from tops of shrubs. **Voice**: Song begins with two or more clear whistles, then a series of trills, often descending. **Did you know?** Vesper Sparrows sing beautifully at dusk, thus the name.

SAVANNAH SPARROW *Passerculus sandwichensis*

Description: 5.25″. **Small, streaked above and below. Short tail,** whitish central crown stripe, and **yellowish eyebrow. Similar Species**: Song Sparrow (page 393) larger, darker brown with long tail. Lincoln's Sparrow (page 395) gray-headed with buff mustache mark, finer breast streaks. Vesper Sparrow (above) has white-edged tail. **Status and Habitat:** Common summer resident throughout in open grassland, farmlands, meadows, salt marsh, and large grassy parks in cities. A few winter. **Behavior**: Forages on ground for seeds and insects. Forms flocks in winter. Male sings from elevated perches. **Voice**: Buzzy song of 2–3 longer notes followed by lower-pitched, less-clear buzzes. Calls include sharp, high but quiet *pik*, thin *tsew*. **Did you know?** Great numbers of Savannah Sparrows from Alaska migrate through our region.

Date & Location Seen: _____

Sooty

Slate-colored

Description: 6.5". Bulky, **plain-faced sparrow with chevron-shaped spots** on whitish breast, reddish brown tail, yellowish lower bill. Two distinct forms in region. Sooty variably dark **chocolate-brown to gray-brown with dense markings below.** Slate-colored **gray on head and back** contrasting with rusty wings and tail; less heavily marked below.

Similar Species: Song Sparrow (page 393) smaller with streaked back, gray eyebrow, and darker bill. Hermit Thrush (page 353) has slender bill, spotted breast.

Status and Habitat: Sooty common migrant and winter resident in region, early September–early May; scarce breeder on a few San Juan Islands and at Cape Flattery. Slate-colored fairly common summer resident in Cascades below subalpine zone; rare in lowlands. Snoqualmie and Stevens passes most accessible sites. Mountain breeding habitat meadow edges near small trees. Wintering in brushy fields and forest edge, including backyards; blackberry thickets and dense tangles preferred.

Behavior: Forages mostly on ground for seeds, insects, and some fruit. Scrapes ground with both feet, jumping forward and kicking back. Migrants sing in fall and spring in lowlands. Visits feeders, especially during snowstorms.

Voice: Song rich, complex, melodic, staccato, and lively. Calls include hard, smacking *tip*.

Did you know? Highly variable across its continent-wide range, Fox Sparrow is sometimes treated as four separate species.

Date & Location Seen: _____

Description: 6″. Streaked brownish above with brown wings. **Dark, dense streaking** usually merges into central spot on whitish breast. **Long, rounded tail pumped in flight. Wide gray eyebrow**, brown crown with gray central stripe, dark mustache mark. JUVENILE: Finely streaked below, no breast spot.

Similar Species: Fox Sparrow (page 391) has plain back and lacks facial stripes. Savannah (page 389) and Lincoln's (page 395) Sparrows paler, shorter-tailed. Swamp Sparrow (rare winter visitor) similar above but plain gray below, with contrasting white throat.

Status and Habitat: Common resident. Most abundant sparrow in region, occurring throughout up to mountain passes and into wooded parts of cities. Prefers shrubs and thicket edge in wetter areas but frequents all semi-open habitats as well as shrubby woodland.

Behavior: Feeds mostly on ground on insects and seeds (including below bird feeders), some fruit. Less prone to flock, in fact, highly territorial in winter, but in high densities in favorable areas. Sings year-round in region, begins nesting in late winter.

Voice: Song begins with several clear notes followed by lower note and jumbled trill. Calls include distinctive nasal *chump*, thin *seet*.

Did you know? Song Sparrows are almost semi-aquatic, feeding on aquatic insects and even small fish as they wade in shallow water at the shore.

Date & Location Seen: _____

Description: 5.25". **Small**, secretive. Streaked above and below. **Buff wash on breast and sides with distinct fine, dark streaks,** sometimes central spot, clear white belly. Short tail, small bill, grayish face with divided brown crown, faint eye-ring, dark eye-line, and **buff mustache mark.**

Similar Species: Smaller and paler than Song Sparrow (page 393), with finer streaks. More reddish than Savannah Sparrow (page 389) and lacks white or yellow eyebrow of that species.

Status and Habitat: Fairly common breeder in open meadows and bogs in Cascades, May–September. In summer, around all mountain passes and higher elevations along North Cascades Highway. Common migrant and fairly common in winter at lower elevations. Prefers wet, brushy places at all seasons, but migrants use variety of habitats, can turn up in backyards in city neighborhoods.

Behavior: Feeds mostly on ground on seeds and insects, in or near cover. Never in flocks but may associate with other sparrows.

Voice: Song fairly long series of bubbly musical trills, generally given only on nesting grounds. Call sharp but soft *tip*, like a subdued Fox Sparrow.

Did you know? Perhaps only a coincidence, but the song of Lincoln's Sparrow sounds much like that of the House Wren, also a dweller of shrubby areas.

Date & Location Seen: _____

Adult

Immature

Description: 6″. Rather long-tailed, richly colored sparrow with **vivid head markings, including white throat** set off from gray cheeks and underparts. Yellow spot before eye. Dark brown back, streaked with black, and white wing-bars. Some adults have tan instead of white eyebrow. IMMATURE: Head stripes dark brown and buffy-gray, some streaking on sides.

Similar Species: White-crowned (page 399) and Golden-crowned (page 401) Sparrows without contrasty white throat, not as richly colored. American Tree and Chipping Sparrows (page 387) smaller, more slender-looking. All other sparrows with streaked and spotted breasts.

Status and Habitat: Uncommon winter visitor throughout low-lands, October–April. Prefers dense shrub thickets.

Behavior: Stays under cover more than White-crowned and Golden-crowned but may come out and feed on seeds in open with these other *Zonotrichia* species. Often seen at feeders in suburbs but darts into shrubbery when disturbed.

Voice: Rich *tsink* in winter; rarely sings sweet, whistled spring song.

Did you know? Bird songs all over the world have been expressed in local languages. This one has been likened to "Old Sam Peabody, Peabody, Peabody" or "Oh sweet Canada, Canada, Canada."

Date & Location Seen: _____

Adult

Immature

Description: 6.25". Fairly large and long-tailed, with **unstreaked gray breast, black and white head stripes, yellowish orange bill.** Faint white wing-bars, streaked back. IMMATURE: **Brown and gray head stripes.** JUVENILE: Streaked breast just out of nest.

Similar Species: Golden-crowned Sparrow (page 401) a bit larger with dusky bill, immature with less-defined head stripes. White-throated Sparrow (page 397) browner, smaller, with clearly marked, bright white throat.

Status and Habitat: Common summer resident, less common in winter. Nests throughout region up to mountain passes. Breeds in open areas, including shrubby woodland edge, parks, and even vegetation strips in city malls. Winters locally in lowlands, mostly in agricultural areas; prefers farms and hedgerows.

Behavior: Forages mostly on ground for insects, seeds, and other plant material. Occasionally flycatches from trees and shrubs. Flocks with other sparrows.

Voice: Song begins with 1–2 whistled calls followed by rhythmic series of buzzy trilled notes—*seeee pretty pretty meeeeee*. Calls include sharp *bink* and high, thin *seet*.

Did you know? Most of our breeding birds winter in California. Those that remain are joined by larger numbers of birds of another subspecies coming from Alaska for the winter. These northern birds have brighter bills and more contrasty gray and rufous back streaking. Their song, sung in spring, also sounds a bit different.

Date & Location Seen: _____

Adult

Immature

Description: 6.75". **Large** and long-tailed, **with unstreaked gray breast** and relatively small conical bill, with dark upper and light lower mandible. Streaked brown above with rather plain head and faint white wing-bars. BREEDING: **Golden crown bordered by black cap**. NONBREEDING, IMMATURE: Lacks black, **finely streaked crown** with hint of gold on forehead.

Similar Species: White-crowned Sparrow (page 399) slightly smaller, with orange-pink bill; adult has black and white head stripes, immature brown and gray stripes. Golden-crowned immature has finer streaks on crown.

Status and Habitat: Common winter resident at lower elevations throughout region. Arrives mid September, departs by mid May. Fall migrants also up into alpine zone in mountains. Brushy places, including suburban neighborhoods.

Behavior: Forages on ground for seeds and insects, often in flocks with other *Zonotrichia* sparrows. Such groups can be surprisingly tame. Also feeds in trees and shrubs on flower buds, especially in spring. Occasionally flycatches.

Voice: Song, often given in spring, a series of several rather sweet whistled notes, one or more extended and trilled (*"look at meeeeee"*). Call notes include thin *seep*, rich, loud *bink*.

Did you know? Golden-crowned and White-crowned Sparrows occasionally hybridize, such hybrids exciting to watch for at feeders!

Date & Location Seen: _____

Oregon Male

Slate-colored Male

Oregon Female

Oregon Juvenile

DARK-EYED JUNCO
Junco hyemalis

Description: 5.75". Sparrow-shaped with short **pink conical bill, white outer tail feathers.** Two distinct subspecies in region. Oregon male with **black hood**, plain brown back, **rusty sides,** white belly; female duller with gray hood. Slate-colored completely **gray**, including sides, with white belly; may be brownish tinge on back.

Similar Species: Only other small ground-feeding songbirds with white outer tail feathers are heavily streaked American Pipit (page 361), Lapland Longspur (page 365), and Vesper Sparrow (page 389), all in wide-open habitats. Juvenile juncos streaked above and below, can be mistaken for sparrow but have white tail edges, pinkish bill.

Status and Habitat: Common resident throughout region. Nests in coniferous and mixed woods, particularly at brushy edges. Increasingly common breeder in well-wooded suburbs, and in migration and winter can appear anywhere. Oregon common year-round, small numbers of Slate-colored appear in winter from Alaska.

Behavior: Flocks forage on ground, also in trees, for seeds and insects. Often scratches at ground with feet. Regular on and beneath bird feeders.

Voice: Trilled song similar to that of Chipping Sparrow but more musical. Most common call sharp *tip*.

Did you know? Oregon and Slate-colored are just two of the many distinctive regional forms of the widely distributed, highly variable Dark-eyed Junco.

Date & Location Seen: _____

Male

Female

Description: 6.5". Compact, with **fairly stout bill.** BREEDING ADULT MALE: Black back, tail, and wings, **yellow and white wing-bars. Bright yellow with scarlet head.** FIRST-YEAR and NONBREEDING MALE: much less red on head. FEMALE: Olive replaces black areas of male, no red on head; back and belly can be gray. Wing-bars reduced but still conspicuous.

Similar Species: Some other birds colored somewhat like female. Female Bullock's Oriole (page 421) with much more pointed bill and longer, orange tail. Warblers and goldfinches smaller.

Status and Habitat: Common summer resident throughout region, May–September. Fairly open coniferous or mixed forest; rarely nests successfully in urban areas. Migrants use varied habitats, can be inconspicuous in canopy. Easiest to spot at forest edges.

Behavior: Gleans methodically in treetops, mostly for insects; occasionally sallies. Also takes fruit, especially in fall. Migrants often move in small flocks.

Voice: Song a short series of slow phrases similar to that of American Robin, but hoarser. Call distinctive *per-dick* (think of it as *pretty*).

Did you know? Recent research has confirmed that the Western Tanager and its near relatives are not members of the tanager family but instead belong to a family of finch-like birds that includes Black-headed Grosbeak (page 407) and Lazuli Bunting (page 409).

Date & Location Seen: _____

Male

Female

Description: 7.25″. Larger than most finches. Plump-looking, with **large conical bill**. ADULT MALE: **Black head**, tail, and wings. **Wings and tail with bold white markings. Breast and rump brownish orange**. FIRST-YEAR MALE: Stripes on head, brown wing feathers. FEMALE: Striped sparrow-like above, rich tawny-brown below, with white wing-bars. Strong **white head stripes.**

Similar Species: Evening Grosbeak (page 437) male with yellow eyebrow, female with plain head. No sparrow with orange breast like female.

Status and Habitat: Common summer resident (May–August) throughout region up to mountain passes. Nests mostly in mature deciduous or mixed forests away from urban areas, but more widespread in migration, often turning up in wooded city yards.

Behavior: Forages in trees for insects, seeds, and berries. Regular at bird feeders with black oil sunflower seeds, especially immatures in fall.

Voice: Song a long, whistled, melodious warble likened to a "drunken robin." Songs discrete, separated by pauses, while robin songs continuous. Distinctive call note, sharp *pik*, often reveals its presence.

Did you know? Both the male and the female Black-headed Grosbeak sing, which is not uncommon among finch-like birds. First-year males, duller versions of adult males, sing and set up territories but don't seem to be good at attracting mates.

Date & Location Seen: _____

Male

Female

Description: 5". Like a **miniature bluebird** but with a sparrow bill. MALE: Blue head and back, orange breast, and white belly; blue-tinged wings and tail; strong **white wing-bars.** FEMALE: Entirely **plain brown**, paler below, with two pale wing-bars.

Similar Species: Western Bluebird (page 349) superficially similar but larger, with slender bill and no wing-bars. Female Lazuli sparrow-like but no hint of dark streaks or spots. Female and juvenile Brown-headed Cowbird (page 419) larger and darker (juvenile has faint wing-bars).

Status and Habitat: Uncommon and local summer resident (May–August) in semi-open brushy areas in lowlands. Singing males in many areas where breeding not documented. Rare migrant elsewhere.

Behavior: Males sing from prominent perches, even high in trees. Most foraging for insects and seeds on ground and in shrubs.

Voice: Song a series of whistled notes, each repeated 2–5 times. Calls a sharp *pik* and buzzy but musical *zink*.

Did you know? First-year male Lazuli Buntings learn their songs from all of the mature males they hear around them when they return to a breeding territory in spring. They adopt phrases from different birds and shuffle them around to produce a new combination. In a few days, they have established their own unique song, and they use it for the rest of their life.

Date & Location Seen: _____

Male

Female

Description: Male 8.5", female 7.25". Medium-sized blackbird with fairly **stout, sharply pointed bill**. MALE: **Glossy black with red "shoulder" patch** (actually at wrist) bordered with yellow-buff. FIRST-YEAR MALE: Red patch paler, spotted; barred and streaked above with brown. FEMALE: Smaller, dark brown above and paler below, **heavily streaked** and with strong **buff eyebrow.**

Similar Species: Other blackbirds lack red patch. Sparrows smaller than female Red-winged Blackbird, with shorter bill.

Status and Habitat: Common resident throughout, up to mountain passes in summer. Breeds at ponds and marshes and along lake shores, less often at bogs and brushy wet meadows. In winter shifts from wetlands to farms, retreats from higher altitudes. Continues to roost in wetlands while feeding at farms and feedlots.

Behavior: Forages mostly on ground for seeds and insects. Visits seed feeders in some areas. Flocks with other blackbirds. During nesting, polygamous males protect their territory with frequent song, aggressively chasing out all intruders. Multiple females breed with males that have productive territories.

Voice: Main song of male *conk a ree*. Calls include *chek* note, female chattering.

Did you know? Red-winged Blackbirds give more than 20 different vocalizations, a reflection of their complex social organization. Males have 18 different calls, females six. Four alarm calls are given by both sexes.

Date & Location Seen: _____

Description: 9″. **Long-billed, short-tailed** member of blackbird family. Prominent white eyebrow and dark eye-line. Back brown, barred and streaked with black. **Bright yellow underparts** with V-shaped black breast band. Sides white, heavily streaked with black. **Outer tail feathers white.** Low flight, often with much gliding.

Similar Species: Similarly shaped European Starling (page 359) lacks yellow underparts and white outer tail feathers. In silhouette, meadowlark with longer legs, perches higher on fence wires.

Status and Habitat: Rare summer resident, uncommon in winter. Mostly gone as breeder; still nests locally in South Sound Prairies, perhaps elsewhere. Winters throughout region in low-elevation meadows and agricultural areas. Fields, prairies, and farms. Some move to wet coastal habitats in winter.

Behavior: Forages on ground for insects and seeds. Probes soil with long, pointed bill, gaping it open to expose food. In winter often in flocks. May perch and sing high in trees, even during migration and winter; also sings from fence wires and ground.

Voice: Song gurgling series of flute-like notes. Calls include *chupp* and rattle; thin, high buzz in flight.

Did you know? The Western Meadowlark is visually almost identical to the Eastern Meadowlark. Noting its different song, John James Audubon recognized that Western Meadowlark was a different species. He named it *neglecta* in Latin because others had overlooked it.

Date & Location Seen: _____

Male

Female

Description: Male 9.5", female 7.75". Large blackbird of marshlands. MALE: Glossy black with bright yellow head and breast, small black mask; conspicuous white wing patch. FIRST-YEAR MALE: Yellow duller and less extensive, no white in wing. FEMALE: Obviously smaller, brown with dark yellowish throat and upper breast, often white speckles on lower breast.

Similar Species: Nothing in region like either sex.

Status and Habitat: Very local breeder, mostly at Joint Base Lewis-McChord and Ridgefield National Wildlife Refuge. Breeds in marshes, using cattails to support nest. Otherwise uncommon migrant in spring or fall anywhere in lowlands. A few in wintering blackbird flocks.

Behavior: Feeds on ground on seeds and insects, entirely insects at breeding marshes, where aquatic insects such as damselflies emerging from the water furnish majority of food. Polygamous, each male attempting to attract multiple females. After breeding, joins mixed flocks of blackbirds at feedlots or in fallow fields.

Voice: Male "song" a harsh and prolonged screeching, hard on the ears. Call *chuck*, deeper than other blackbirds.

Did you know? Red-winged Blackbirds arrive in migration early in spring and set up territories. Yellow-headed Blackbirds arrive later, but because they are larger, they dominate the redwings and push them out of favored territories.

Date & Location Seen: _____

Male

Female

Description: 9". Medium-sized blackbird with **medium-length pointed bill** and fairly long tail. MALE: Black in distance but actually **glossy dark bluish green with purplish iridescent head, light yellow eye**. FEMALE: **Drab brown** with slight iridescence on wings, dark eye.

Similar Species: Red-winged Blackbird (page 411) not as plain; female streaked, male with patch of red. Brown-headed Cowbird (page 419) smaller, bill finch-like. Rusty Blackbird, rare winter visitor, has light eye in both sexes and brownish feather edgings in male.

Status and Habitat: Common but local resident in region. Patchily distributed around cities; more easily found in agricultural areas. Pastures, feed lots, urban parking lots, and other open places.

Behavior: Forages mostly walking on ground, takes insects but also seeds and waste grain. Probably eats almost anything in mall parking lots. After breeding, flocks with other blackbirds and starlings at feedlots, roosts in nearby trees.

Voice: Courting male has high-pitched *kseee* song. Year-round nasal *check* note.

Did you know? Nest-site selection by Brewer's Blackbirds varies greatly depending on local availability. They may build their nests in trees, on plant stalks over water, in low shrubs, on the ground in high grass, or even on rocky ledges.

Date & Location Seen: _____

Male

Female

Description: 7". Small blackbird with **stubby conical bill** and relatively **short tail**. MALE: Black with **brown head**. FEMALE: Smaller, **plain gray-brown**, lighter below, with vague streaks. JUVENILE: Similar to female but paler, streaking more distinct.

Similar Species: Short bill and brown head distinguish male from other blackbirds. Female smaller and shorter-billed than Brewer's Blackbird (page 419), plainer than sparrows and finches.

Status and Habitat: Common summer resident throughout region in most wooded habitats, including parks and neighborhoods. Most depart in winter, but small numbers persist in flocks, especially at feedlots. In migration and winter prefers fields and farms.

Behavior: Feeds on ground on seeds and insects. A brood parasite, not building its own nest but instead laying eggs in other birds' nests. In breeding season groups of males display with odd postures and spread wings, then chase females. Flocks with other blackbirds after breeding. Often feeds around livestock to capture flushed insects; naive juveniles will do the same with people.

Voice: Male gives gurgling squeaks in display. Female rattles. Flight call thin, high whistle. Juvenile begs from host species with *cheep*, given frequently.

Did you know? Brown-headed Cowbirds, once restricted to plains habitats, invaded forested regions as land was cleared for agriculture, settlement, and lumber production. Cowbird brood parasitism is now implicated in the decline of many forest songbirds.

Date & Location Seen: _____

Male

Female

Description: 7". Slim-looking with **sharply pointed bill** and **long tail.** MALE: **Orange** with black cap, back, wings, eye-line, narrow bib, and center of tail. **Large white wing patch.** FEMALE: Duller, mostly gray-olive with **orange wash** on head and throat, whitish belly, and **white wing-bars.** FIRST-YEAR MALE: Like female but with black throat.

Similar Species: Male unmistakable in region. Size and bill shape distinguish female from tanagers, grosbeaks, and warblers.

Status and Habitat: Uncommon summer resident (May–August) in lowlands. Typically in riparian woodland along rivers but also open groves, parks, and suburban neighborhoods where large deciduous trees, especially cottonwoods, are present. Likely to be found anywhere along larger rivers.

Behavior: Forages in foliage of trees and shrubs for insects, fruits, and nectar from flowers. Weaves light-colored hanging bag-shaped nest in outer limbs, concealed by leaves but obvious in winter. Sometimes visits hummingbird feeders.

Voice: Song a series of rich, medium-pitched whistles and chattering. Typical calls include rolling chatter.

Did you know? With their sharp bills, Bullock's Orioles can pierce the eggs of Brown-headed Cowbirds, a brood parasite, and remove them from their nest. The cowbird eggs would otherwise hatch, and the young would grow rapidly and usually outcompete the oriole young.

Date & Location Seen: _____

Description: 6.5". Ground-dwelling dark finch with yellow bill. Plumage **dark brown** with darker streaks on back and **pinkish overtones** on rump and belly. Rather long wings with broad whitish to pinkish feather edges. Breeding birds with **head mostly gray,** with black crown and throat. Rare migrants from north a subspecies with body color extending farther up on head.

Similar Species: No other sparrowlike ground-feeding bird is colored like a rosy-finch.

Status and Habitat: Fairly common summer resident in alpine zone of high Cascades and Olympics. Mount Rainier best chance for observation. Rare winter visitor, especially near coast. Most breeding birds drop down to eastern Washington for winter, but a few come into our region, augmented by a few more from Alaska breeding populations.

Behavior: Forages on ground for seeds of herbaceous plants all year, also insects and spiders in summer. Nests in rock crevices and roosts in them at night on both breeding and wintering grounds. After breeding, usually in nomadic flocks that travel over the countryside, easily flying in strong winds.

Voice: Most common call buzzy *chew.*

Did you know? Rosy-finches and other alpine birds commonly seek insects and spiders that have fallen onto snow banks and become torpid.

Date & Location Seen: _____

_____

423

**Pine Grosbeak
Male**

**Pine Grosbeak
Female**

**Common Redpoll
Male**

Description: 9". Robin-sized finch with stubby black bill, **white wing-bars,** and **long tail.** MALE: **Rosy-pink head, back, breast, and rump.** Gray sides and belly. White wing-bars. FEMALE: All gray except **yellowish or rust-colored head. Similar Species**: All reddish finches much smaller. Female vaguely like Townsend's Solitaire (page 351) but different bill and behavior. **Status and Habitat**: Breeds in conifer forests near treeline in North Cascades and south to Mount Rainier. In winter uncommon visitor to lowlands, more likely in north. Wintering birds in parks with fruiting trees. **Behavior**: Males sing from tops of small conifers. After breeding, usually in small flocks looking for seeds, buds, and fruit. **Voice**: Loud warbled song. Call a characteristic double whistle. **Did you know?** Like many birds of the far north, Pine Grosbeaks are charmingly tame.

COMMON REDPOLL *Acanthis flammea*

Description: 4.5". Tiny finch with sharply pointed bill, streaked brown all over and with **red crown**. Male has **pinkish-red breast,** lacking in female. **Similar Species**: Smaller and sharper-billed than other red finches, Purple (page 427) and House (page 429). Pine Siskin (page 433) similar but no red. **Status and Habitat:** Erratic winter visitor to woodland with favored trees, more likely in northern part. Absent some years. **Behavior**: Small flocks feed on birch and alder seeds in countryside or suburbs. **Voice**: Calls a musical *tuwee* and hard *chif chif* heard from feeding flocks. **Did you know?** Several types of redpolls occupy northern latitudes, but recent genetic analysis indicates they are all a single species.

Date & Location Seen: ─────────────────

Male

Female

Description: 5.5". Stocky finch with **stout bill** and **short, notched tail**. MALE: **Raspberry-red** on head and breast, extending to flanks and infusing finely streaked brown back. Unstreaked below. FEMALE, FIRST-YEAR MALE: Brownish olive with blurry streaks on whitish underparts. **Broad white eyebrow**.

Similar Species: House Finch (page 429) with longer tail, male more orange-red with streaks on sides and belly. Female lacks broad white eyebrow.

Status and Habitat: Locally fairly common resident throughout rural and semi-rural parts of region. Uncommon in cites but avoids dense forests. Prefers mixed woods, coniferous forest edge, and semi-open areas with fruiting trees. Some local movement as birds appear at urban feeders spring and fall.

Behavior: Forages on fruits, seeds, buds, and some insects. In flocks outside nesting season. More arboreal than House Finch but also feeds on ground. Visits bird feeders, sometimes in pairs.

Voice: Song a series of warbled notes without harsh ending of House Finch. Calls include muffled whistle, sharp *pik* given in flight.

Did you know? Purple Finches have undergone serious decline in urbanized Puget Sound, often attributed to competition with the recently arrived and more adaptable House Finch. Other factors such as forest fragmentation and habitat change may also be involved.

Date & Location Seen: _____

Male

Female

HOUSE FINCH
Haemorhous mexicanus

Description: 5.5". Sparrow-sized finch with long, slightly notched tail. **Bill short and rounded.** MALE: **Red** (yellow or orange in some individuals) on crown, breast, and rump; **streaks on belly and flanks.** FEMALE: Brownish gray without red. Blurry streaks on gray-white breast and belly. **No strong facial pattern.**

Similar Species: Purple Finch (page 427) more robust, adult male without streaks on lower breast, female with broad white eyebrow. Pine Siskin (page 433) smaller and slender-billed.

Status and Habitat: Common year-round resident throughout, more common in lowlands but few up to mountain passes. Urban neighborhoods, parks, suburbs, farms, and woodland edge. Avoids dense forest.

Behavior: Often nests and feeds in urban yards. Usually forages in flocks on ground for weed seeds or in trees for seeds, berries, flowers, and buds. Regular at sunflower feeders.

Voice: Song a series of cheery warbling notes usually ending with harsh note. Call loud, sweet *chirp*.

Did you know? Native to deserts, scrublands, grasslands, and open forests of Mexico and the Southwest, House Finches extended their range as land was cleared for human settlement, first reaching the Puget Sound Region in the 1950s. Introduced to New York City in the 1940s, House Finches have now spread throughout eastern North America as well.

Date & Location Seen: _____

Red Crossbill
Male

Female

White-winged Crossbill
Male

Female

Description: 5.75" / 6". Compact finches with **short tail; bill heavy with crossed tips. Red** male brick red, younger individuals orange or yellowish. Female olive-yellow. **White-winged** with vivid **broad white wing-bars.** Male **pink**, wings and tail black; female greenish. Juvenile of both dull and streaked.

Similar Species: Purple (page 427) and House (page 429) Finches streaked like juvenile but smaller, longer-tailed. Pine Grosbeak (page 425) larger with white wing-bars, stubbier bill.

Status and Habitat: Red fairly common resident throughout region in coniferous forest. Erratic and nomadic, breeds at any time except late winter. Localities and abundance vary with cone crops. **White-winged** rather rare visitor, more likely high in mountains but may reach lowlands, usually in spruce trees.

Behavior: Flocks seek productive conifers (spruce for **White-winged**, most species for **Red**), pry cones open, and extract seeds. Also at times eat buds, other seeds, and insects. Like other finches, attracted to water.

Voice: Song a rapid series of hard chirps and warbles, not often heard. Both call mostly in flight, **Red** a musical *kip kip* or *veet veet*, **White-winged** a drier *chiff chiff.*

Did you know? Eight different forms of Red Crossbill in North America vary in bill size and in subtleties of their call notes. Each roams about in search of the cone type that its bill is best adapted to open.

Date & Location Seen: _____

Pine Siskin

Lesser Goldfinch
Male

Female

Description: 4.5". **Small finch** with **slender conical bill, streaked all over.** Yellow on wings and tail, yellow wing stripe especially evident in flight. **Similar Species**: Smaller than House (page 429) and Purple (page 427) Finches. Common Redpoll (page 425) has red cap. **Status and Habitat**: Common woodland resident throughout but nomadic and cyclic in abundance and can be very scarce some years. **Behavior**: Feeds especially on red alder seeds in winter, also on weed seeds and at thistle and sunflower feeders. Large, compact flocks swirl noisily when alarmed. **Voice**: Song a jumble of husky twitters and trills. Calls include rising *zreeee* and high, sharp *di di di*. **Did you know?** In spring, Pine Siskins often glean insects from large limbs, feeding somewhat like a nuthatch.

LESSER GOLDFINCH *Spinus psaltria*

Description: 4.5". **Small finch** with short dark bill, white wing-bar, and white patch at base of flight feathers. MALE: **greenish upperparts with black cap,** yellow underparts. FEMALE: olive-green above, dull yellowish below. **Similar Species**: American Goldfinch (page 435) with darker wings and more conspicuous wing-bars. **Status and Habitat:** Uncommon resident in southern part of region, slowly spreading northward. No guaranteed breeding sites, but watch for it at feeders anywhere. Often in oak woodland but wanders widely. **Behavior**: Like American Goldfinch, feeding on weed seeds. **Voice**: Call musical *tee-you*, song a jumble of whistled and tinkly notes. **Did you know?** This species extends southward to northern South America, males of populations to the south with black backs.

Date & Location Seen: _____

Male

Nonbreeding

Female

Description: 4.5". Variable plumage with **prominent white wing-bars** on black wings, white rump and undertail, and black tail with white edgings. **Short conical bill,** pinkish in summer. BREEDING: Male **bright yellow** with **black forehead.** Female dull yellow, olive on back. NONBREEDING: Dull gray-brown all over, yellowish on head. JUVENILE: Browner on back with buff wing-bars.

Similar Species: Conical bill distinguishes from warblers, lack of streaks from sparrows and other finches. See Lesser Goldfinch (page 433).

Status and Habitat: Fairly common resident throughout region, but many birds migrate south; may be difficult to find in winter. Nests in open woodland or open areas with some deciduous trees, including farmland. Less common in cities but frequents neighborhoods with some open areas such as weedy lots. Moves into more open country in winter.

Behavior: Gregarious, with flocks most evident late summer and fall. Late nesting coincides with summer seed production. Eats small seeds, especially of weedy herbaceous plants such as thistles (favors thistle feeders), also in trees such as alder and birch.

Voice: Song a long jumble of high, repeated twitters and phrases. Calls include *per chic o ree*, mostly given in flight, and thin *tweee*.

Did you know? The American Goldfinch is the state bird of Washington, as well as Iowa and New Jersey.

Date & Location Seen: _____

_____

Male

Female

Description: 7″. Plump-looking short-tailed finch with **big, conical chartreuse bill** (paler in winter). Black wings and tail, former with **large white patches**. MALE: **Bright yellow eyebrow.** Brown head and breast grade to yellow wing coverts and belly. FEMALE: Brownish gray with yellowish wash, black mustache marks, much white in wings and tail.

Similar Species: Black-headed Grosbeak (page 407) lacks yellow eyebrow of male, plain head of female. American Goldfinch (page 435) much smaller.

Status and Habitat: Fairly common resident throughout region but more irregular in winter. Breeds in coniferous and mixed forests, more common as nester in mountains. Easiest to find in May, even in cities.

Behavior: Gregarious outside breeding season. Roams the countryside in flocks, foraging together mostly in trees, on seeds and buds including maple and ash. Also eats insects (abundant at spruce budworm outbreaks) and fruit, comes to ground for gravel. Voracious flocks visit bird feeders.

Voice: Apparently no well-developed song. Calls strident, ringing *tcheer* and short trill given often by flocking birds.

Did you know? Their scientific and common names come from the erroneous notion that Evening Grosbeaks are most active after sunset, dating back to the first scientific description of the species in 1825.

Date & Location Seen: _____

Male

Female

Description: 5.75". An Old World sparrow, not closely related to native sparrows. Short-tailed, with streaked upperparts, **unstreaked** dingy gray breast, and one white wing-bar. MALE: Gray crown, **black bill, spectacles, and bib**, chestnut sides of neck, and rich brown upperparts. Colors duller in fall and early winter. FEMALE: **Light buff eyebrow and back stripes.**

Similar Species: No native sparrows with male head pattern or buffy eyebrow of female. Finches of similar size streaked.

Status and Habitat: Common resident throughout region, mostly in lowlands and mostly near human habitation. Cities, suburbs, and farms.

Behavior: Feeds on ground, often in flocks, on seeds and insects. Roosts communally and noisily in thick shrubbery. Competes aggressively for cavity nest sites, much to detriment of native species. Regular at bird feeders. Prolific breeders, with an average of three clutches per year, may produce 20 chicks total.

Voice: Repeated series of *chirrup* notes. Chirping call often given by many birds simultaneously, creating surprising din. Also rattles in excitement.

Did you know? Male House Sparrows get brighter as they begin nesting, not as a result of molting but through feather wear that reveals the attractive colors beneath. The species was introduced from Europe in the 1850s to parks in New York City and rapidly spread across North America. It is now cosmopolitan.

Date & Location Seen: _____

Acknowledgments, Photographer Credits

I would like to thank Christina Duchesne Morse for inviting me to lead this project to update and revise **Birds of the Puget Sound Region.** Christina was a student of mine long ago at the University of Washington, and who would have thought our lives would intersect again like this forty years later? It has been a pleasure working with her. I also appreciate team member Christina Merwin's skills at setting up the book design and placing the images so well on the pages. Both Christinas worked with efficiency and grace. I was pleased to work again with Brian E. Small, our Photo Editor, whose beautiful photos make the book a joy to behold and use in the field. I deeply acknowledge my wife Netta Smith, who encourages and supports me in every way through projects such as this one.

Brian E. Small worked as the Photo Editor for this book. He has provided over 400 images from his vast collection of high quality wildlife photographs for use in this guide. All remaining images were provided by a select handful of North America's finest bird photographers. Their contributions are as follows:

The letters following the page numbers refer to the position of the photograph on that page (T = top, B = bottom, L = left, R = right, M = middle, N = inset).

Lee Barnes: 240. **Glenn Bartley**: 28T, 64N, 160T, 190T, 196T, 198T, 202T, 206T, 206B, 208T, 208B, 224T, 228T, 364T, 364B. **Joe Fuhrman**: 66B, 94N, 108B, 244. **Steve Mlodinow**: 254T. **Alan Murphy**: 60T, 82T, 108T, 200B, 266B, 318T, 430B, 430BN, 384N, 384B. **Dennis Paulson**: 102B, 106B, 106BN, 110T, 132BR, 180B, 194BR, 200N, 210T, 220M, 224B, 258B. **Jim Pruske:** 232, 302T, 330T, 356T, 356B, 410B. **David Quady:** 200T. **David Salem:** 48N. **Larry Sansone**: 202B, 204B, 314BL. **Jacob Spendelow**: 66T, 250T. **Bob Steele**: 24T, 38TN, 84B, 254B, 278T, 292B, 306T, 316B, 326, 358BL. **Glen Tepke:** 320TL. **Jim Zipp**: 138L, 138R, 142T, 142B, 144T, 144B.

440

Index/Checklist of Puget Sound Region Birds

Use this checklist to keep a record of the birds you have seen.
Bold numbers are for the main Species Account page.

442

444

Other Species Seen

_____

_____

_____

_____

_____

About The Authors

DENNIS PAULSON Now retired from the Directorship of the Slater Museum of Natural History, University of Puget Sound, Dennis is the author of nine natural-history books, including *Shorebirds of the Pacific Northwest* and *Shorebirds of North America: The Photographic Guide*. He has studied and taught about the natural history of Washington since 1967. He is a founding member of the Washington Ornithological Society and the primary instructor for Seattle Audubon Society's Master Birders program.

BOB MORSE Bob has seen over 850 species of birds in the United States, 438 species in Washington State, and has written/published twelve bird books. With Christina Morse, they operate the R.W. Morse Company which publishes and sells regional bird guides.

TOM AVERSA Co-author of four books on Pacific Northwest birds, studied birds while specializing in raptors at Woodland Park Zoo in Seattle and served on the Washington Bird Records Committee. Major interests include behavior, status, distribution and comparison of racial variation in wide-ranging species. Tom relocated to Maine in 2010 with his wife Cheryl where he teaches about wildlife and captive wildlife care as an adjunct instructor at Unity College. Other strong interests include music, film, and conservation of the natural world.

HAL OPPERMAN Hal has written, edited, and contributed to numerous publications and online resources on birds and birding in the Pacific Northwest. A native of Illinois, he completed his undergraduate studies in biology at Knox College and field stations in Colorado and Montana and holds a doctorate in art history from the University of Chicago. He moved to Seattle to join the University of Washington faculty in 1967. His research and teaching focus on representations of animals and nature in art.